**Published by
Visibility Enterprises**

The Publicity Manual

THE PUBLICITY MANUAL

by

Kate Kelly

Fourth Edition

Copyright © 1983, 1981, 1979 by Kate Kelly

Published by Visibility Enterprises,
11 West 81st Street, New York, N.Y. 10024

Library of Congress Catalog Card Number:
79-55946

International Standard Book Number:
0-9603740-1-9

Printed in the United States of America

THE PUBLICITY MANUAL

Table of Contents

STARTING UP...1

    Chapter I: About Publicity.............................3

        What Publicity Can Do For You......................4

        Why The Media Needs You............................5

        How To Start......................................7

        Your Publicity Budget.............................8

        Budgeting Time....................................8

        Publicity Breeds Publicity........................9

THE BASICS..11

    Chapter II: Planning Your Press Release Content...........12

        Who is Your Audience?.............................12

        What Media Do They Follow?........................13

        What Do You Have To Say?..........................17

        Transforming the Background Release
           into a News Release............................24

        Work Sheet for Planning Your Press Release........25

    Chapter III: How To Write a Press Release.................26

        The Format..26

        The Writing Style.................................30

        Typing It Up......................................32

        Reproducing Your Release..........................32

        Sending It Out....................................34

        Summary Guidelines for Writing a Press Release.....35

        How To Work With a Writer:
           For Those Who Prefer Additional Help...........38

THE BASICS   (continued)

Chapter IV: How To Take Advantage of
Publicity Opportunities.......................40

How To Announce News of a Product or Service......40

How To Plan and Announce Special Events...........46

How To Make the Most of Company News..............65

How To Get Publicity From News
That's Under Your Nose.......................75

How To Maximize Your News By Being "Timely".......81

Your Viewpoint as News: Letters To The Editor......87

Chapter V: Other Types of Press Material 89

The Tip Sheet...90

The Biography Press Release.........................94

Cover Letters.......................................97

The Press Kit.......................................101

Chapter VI: The Importance of Photographs................103

Who Will Take the Photograph?.......................104

What Makes a Good Picture?..........................105

Photos for Product Publicity........................107

Photo Coverage of an Event..........................107

The Portrait Shot...................................109

Permission to Use a Photograph......................110

Ordering Prints.....................................111

The Caption...111

THE MEDIA..113

Chapter VII: Working With the Press......................115

The Contact Process.................................115

Respect Their Situation.............................116

Who Should Receive Your Material?...................119

How To Attract Press Attention......................120

Phoning the Press...................................121

THE MEDIA

Chapter VII: Working With the Press (continued)

How To Time Your Press Material....................123

How To Develop a Press List.......................124

Chapter VIII: Specifics About the Various Media Outlets....126

Newspapers..126

Magazines...127

Trade Publications................................128

Association Publications..........................129

Community Press...................................129

Wire Services.....................................129

Syndicated Services...............................130

Radio and Television..............................131

The Columnist, The Critic and
        The Freelance Writer......................132

Chapter IX: The Interview and After...............137

How To Handle an Interview........................137

Interview Results.................................139

How To Find Out if Your Publicity
        Becomes a Story...........................140

Building a Relationship with a
        Member of the Media.......................141

Being Persistent Pays Off.........................142

YOUR IMAGE..145

Chapter X: How You and Your Company Can Be
        Viewed Positively By Others...............148

Your Personal Image...............................148

How To Be Viewed as an Expert in Your Field.......150

The Physical Appearance of Your Company...........151

Your Staff..153

Public Relations and the Telephone................156

Putting Your Publicity To Work To
        Further Your Image........................157

YOUR IMAGE (continued)

Chapter XI: How and When to Hire an
        Outside Public Relations Firm....................159
    How to Select the Best Firm for
        Your Company...................................160
    What Kind of Fees Can You Expect?..................163
    What Results Can You Expect?......................166
    Establishing the Relationship.....................167

RESOURCES..169
    Press List Resources..............................169
    Other Aids...173
    Sample Chart for Tracking Your Publicity..........175
    Frequently Asked Questions........................178

*   *   *

Starting Up

STARTING UP

Visibility means business.

That's what I've found to be true while working with business owners, professionals and people from the nonprofit sector whom I teach and counsel in workshops and seminars on publicity techniques.

Those who have taken my course were there to learn how to increase their business and enhance their image through free media exposure. They preferred not to hire a public relations professional, and they didn't have to. By attending a publicity workshop, they learned how to achieve visibility themselves.

The results? They've been gratifying. Those who have applied the techniques given in the workshops have gone on to receive exposure on radio and television and in local and national newspapers and magazines. Though what this exposure does for entrepreneurs in terms of image cannot readily be measured, something else can: their resulting increase in business.

From these real-life experiences and my own background

in public relations, I put my knowledge and materials together in The Publicity Manual to enable people like you to do what workshop attendees have done: take full advantage of the many opportunities there are for getting free media exposure.

The Publicity Manual gives you all the tools you'll need to run your own publicity program. Among other things, you'll be learning:

-What publicity can do for you.

-How to develop the news potential of your business or organization in order to attract media attention.

-How to write and use publicity materials such as press releases, biographies, tip sheets and photographs.

-How to announce special events, activities, promotions and new products and services.

-How to contact the media--television, radio, newspapers and magazines--and get results.

-How to achieve personal visibility.

-How to promote a positive image for you and your business or organization.

In addition, my techniques are easy to learn and can be implemented by spending only a few minutes each day or several hours each month.

The skills and methods in this book, confidence in yourself and your business and your firm resolve to set aside time for a publicity program will put you on the road to success. I wish you well.

Chapter I

ABOUT PUBLICITY

Publicity may take the form of a story on the evening
television news, a radio interview, a mention in the community
calendar of your neighborhood newspaper or a full-length
article in a newspaper or magazine. It is free media exposure.
You provide a reporter, editor or producer with basic information
about your business or service, and they decide how best to
use the material within their program or publication--anything
from a brief mention to a lengthy article or interview may
result.

One of the special benefits of publicity is that, in
effect, it is an editorial recommendation--an unbiased opinion--
saying that you are good: "I found this worthy of notice,"
is what the reporter is saying. Obviously, a recommendation
from a member of the press whom the reader or viewer trusts can
often carry more weight than an ad which was paid for and
written by the company itself. One literary agent claims that
an author interview on a local television talk show will sell
more books than a full-page newspaper ad. And of course, the

ad costs money while the interview is free.

If you were to try to calculate the dollar value of publicity for your product, service or business, you'd be astounded at the figures. For example, a 90-second story on the television news in New York--if bought as advertising time--would be worth thousands of dollars!

Calculate it yourself for your own local media. Pick up a newspaper or magazine and find an article that mentions a business, product or service. Measure the space of the article vs. an ad. You may even want to call the publication's sales department to learn the actual cost of the space. The same comparison can be made with radio and television time. After doing these calculations, you'll realize the staggering value of free publicity!

The key to generating publicity for your business is discovering what about your company or organization might be of interest to the public. That's what will make you "news" for the press to report on, and we'll fully discuss this in "The Basics."

WHAT PUBLICITY CAN DO FOR YOU

The overall effect of publicity is visibility--an awareness, recognition and identification by the public of you and your business. With publicity, you're building an image and attracting attention. It can't help but provide you with an edge over your competition. It also helps establish you as an authority and a leader in your field.

Good publicity about a business, product or service
increases the public's knowledge of it, helps create a desire
for it and adds to the public confidence in it. For example,
a reader may have noticed a certain product in an ad or on
display in a shop window, but she has not yet bought the item.
Then she reads an article mentioning it. The article reinforces
her interest in the product by giving her confidence in her
attraction to it. The publicity should also provide her with
the motivation to finally act on her impulse and buy it.

Many business owners I've worked with rely on publicity
and good word-of-mouth to bring them the majority of their
customers and clients. Personal service businesses, particularly,
find that advertising simply isn't as effective as publicity
is for their line of work--people want to hear about a personal
service from a friend or read about it in a magazine or
newspaper before giving it a try.

WHY THE MEDIA NEEDS YOU

You'd be amazed at how heavily newspapers, magazines
and radio and television stations rely on publicity. They need
to hear from many, many sources--including you--in order to
put together the broad spectrum of news stories they cover
regularly.

Try thumbing through a newspaper and noticing where the
stories come from. Aside from the results of an election or
reporting on a major event such as the descent of Skylab or
a local fire, most of the news comes through public relations

sources. When an article refers to "the presidential spokes-
man" or a "corporate spokesperson" that's nothing but publicity.

On the fashion page, the fall fashion collection may be
"news," but in essence, it's a public relations event for the
entire industry. The reason new collections are announced so
formally is to give the media something new to report so that
we, the public, will desire--and buy--what is being touted
as the "latest in fashion."

Where do you fit in with all this? You're news, too. All
you need to do is develop the news potential of your business.
(And I'll tell you how later.) What's more, you may have a
distinct advantage because you're not being slicked up and
packaged by "formula P.R." developed by someone who has been
promoting your type of business for the last twenty years.

The <u>success</u> of many business owners who do their own
publicity stems from their <u>sincerity</u> and their <u>firm belief</u>
in themselves and their businesses. The same is true for
nonprofit organizations. Staffed by committed individuals,
organizations often learn that no one sells the cause better
than their own staff does. This sincerity comes across,
and reporters, editors and producers often respond to it.
They're used to being approached by P.R. professionals who handle
many clients and who simply can't have the same vested interest
in a project as you have. After all, <u>who can convey the strengths
of your business or organization better than you can?</u>

HOW TO START

There is absolutely nothing difficult about doing your own publicity. It takes a little time to prepare the proper written material, and after that, all that is required is organization and common sense.

To get started, I strongly recommend that you read The Publicity Manual from cover to cover. This will provide you with the background you'll need to run your own publicity program. Later you'll find that a quick reference to the appropriate section will remind you of the steps to take for different situations.

Once you've read the book, you'll need to devote time to preparing your written material. As you'll read in "The Basics," I strongly recommend preparation of a general press release giving background information on your business or organization. Then your initial approach to the media can be to send out that basic press release.

Later on, you may be seeking publicity for a special event, a new product or service, a staff promotion or some type of community activity--all of which are discussed in "The Basics"--and I advise you to try them one at a time. When you've gotten as much mileage out of one type of press release as you think you can, then it's time to move on to the next idea.

Remember, your publicity program needs steady application-- not a hard push. If you take on too much at once and let it become burdensome, you may soon feel overwhelmed and discouraged.

That's not necessary. Try one type of press release at a time, and move on to the next only when you feel ready. You'll soon see the results!

YOUR PUBLICITY BUDGET

How much will your publicity program cost? An insignificant amount of your total business budget. <u>A very effective publicity campaign can be run with money spent only on stamps, envelopes and press release copying costs</u>.

Sometimes a business owner may feel that participating in an event such as a street festival or donating a product or service to a worthy cause may net worthwhile press coverage. If you choose to do these things, then your costs will go up accordingly. However, your plans for this type of publicity event can be entirely based on what you can afford.

Regardless of what you spend, always remember that the exposure you get may well be worth hundreds or thousands of dollars!

BUDGETING TIME

If you're like most of the people I work with, you'll probably feel that more difficult than budgeting money for publicity is budgeting time. I cannot stress enough how important it is that you set up some sort of regular schedule for doing publicity. If the techniques in The Publicity Manual are to be effective, you've got to <u>set aside some time on a daily, weekly or monthly basis</u> for putting your program into action.

Some people prefer to devote one to two full days per month to work on their publicity. They'll prepare and mail out thirty to fifty press releases at that time. Then the rest of the month can be devoted to business as usual with a few minutes allotted for follow-ups and interviews when members of the media respond.

Others prefer a more regular schedule, spending a couple of hours each week sending out a few press releases and following up with phone calls on the ones that were mailed the week before.

And some entrepreneurs who are just launching their businesses devote as much as 40 to 50 percent of their time to publicity. Until there are customers to fill one's time, what better use of the day is there than working to achieve the visibility which will bring in business?

No matter how you decide to allot your time, the important thing is to do so. Whether a once-a-week or once-a-month basis seems best, block it out on your calendar. Then make sure daily drudgery doesn't get in the way. <u>To make your publicity campaign an effective one, you're going to have to make it a priority</u>.

PUBLICITY BREEDS PUBLICITY

Once you get started, you'll soon see that publicity breeds publicity. The media is constantly seeking new material, and often <u>their best resource for finding new information is other press stories</u>. One business owner had a short article about her business appear in a neighborhood

newspaper. Within a week she received a phone call from a
radio talk show host who lived in her neighborhood. He said
he had enjoyed the story and wanted to devote a half-hour radio
program to an interview with her!

It all comes back to visibility. <u>The more visible you
become, the more desirable you are to all</u>--including the
media.

But you know how important visibility is going to be to
you. Let's just get started on the material by moving ahead
to "The Basics."

The Basics

THE BASICS

"The Basics" is your encyclopedia of publicity tools.
In it, you'll find complete information on how to prepare
your background press release--the written piece which will
explain what your business is and why it's of special interest.
We'll closely examine both content and format.

In addition, the section contains a wealth of ideas for
many types of promotions as well as an explanation of the
written material appropriate for each occasion. (Each publicity idea discussed is followed by examples of the written
material.) As you read Chapter IV, "How To Take Advantage
of Publicity Opportunities" remember that you need only attempt
one promotion at a time. Read the whole chapter, but when
it comes time to send out that type of press release, you
can return to the section for a reminder of the details.

The section concludes with a discussion of publicity
photographs--a necessity for some types of businesses and
an option for others.

Chapter II

PLANNING YOUR PRESS RELEASE CONTENT

The most important step in getting your publicity campaign underway is preparing the written material which tells about you and your business or organization.

But before writing anything down, a few conclusions need to be reached. In order to develop material for your press release, it's a good idea to return to the hopes and dreams you've had for your business and consider how those ideas might best be conveyed to others. In the process, we'll also need to answer two questions:

- Who is your audience?
- What do you want them to know about your business or organization?

Once you have these answers, the foundation for your publicity program will be solidly established.

WHO IS YOUR AUDIENCE?

Who do you want to reach through publicity?

Take a minute and pretend that with the snap of your fingers you could have the undivided attention of several segments of the population. Who would these people be?

Or if you had an unlimited advertising budget, to whom would you direct your advertising?

Suburban homemakers? Theatre-goers? Bank presidents? General contractors? Teenagers? Middle-class families? Coin collectors? Civic leaders in your community?

Of course, to answer this, you should be identifying who your past, present and potential customers (or for non-profit groups--contributors) are. Other groups whom you might like to tell about your business or organization might include competitors and professional peers as well as "opinion makers" such as civic leaders or people active in your industry or profession who are known for spreading the word about matters they believe in.

(For your convenience, a work sheet for these questions is provided at the end of this chapter on page 25.)

WHAT MEDIA DO THEY FOLLOW?

Now, let's consider what media these groups are likely to read, watch or listen to. Again, if you were placing ads directed to these people, where would you advertise?

You'll probably have a separate media list for each of the groups you think of. For example, the trade publication for your field will be a good way to reach your competitors and professional peers while the local newspaper may be the best medium to reach your current and potential customers or contributors.

If you have any doubts as to the media followed, it will be worth taking an informal survey by chatting with various people to see what publications they read and what programs they watch or listen to. The ones they mention should be added to your media list.

By identifying your audience and the media they are likely

to follow, you have already <u>streamlined your publicity program</u> <u>because you have now set priorities</u>. You know what programs and publications will be the most important to you, so your efforts can now be concentrated toward achieving publicity in those media outlets which are of the most value.

Some examples may further clarify this:

To a couple opening a new seafood restaurant, the <u>local</u> programs and publications will be the most important, because these are the media followed by <u>residents of the community</u> where the restaurant is located. The people who live and work nearby are the ones who can provide the owners with the business needed to pay the bills. At this time, regional and national publicity is of little value to the restaurant owners, because the majority of those audiences cannot become customers for geographic reasons. Eventually, the emphasis could change, and the owners might attempt to establish a statewide reputation for their seafood dishes. But for now, it's the <u>local people</u> <u>whom they need to reach</u> to build business.

A manufacturer who has just developed a new type of knitting machine which will be distributed through retail outlets nationwide may have two different audiences in mind. First, he may need to <u>generate wholesale interest</u> in the product in order to increase the number of outlets carrying the knitting machine. <u>Trade publicity</u> will be important here. The manufacturer will need to seek out the industry newspapers and magazines read by craft and hobby buyers for retail stores. (The "Resources" section mentions books which would list such trade publications.)
Simultaneously, the manufacturer may want to begin <u>generating consumer interest</u> in the machine, so he will look for <u>national publications</u> read by homemakers and craftspeople.

Aside from the craft, sewing and hobby magazines, publications such as Woman's Day and McCall's have sections devoted to new craft or sewing ideas, and their readers might be interested in the knitting machine. Though obviously, craftspeople do watch television and listen to radio, the electronic media would not be the most efficient way to reach them. Unless a program has a segment devoted to new or unusual products, it is usually more difficult to place product publicity here. The exception would be with a product which has earth-shattering news value or if the product spokesperson happens to be Farrah Fawcett or Bruce Jenner.

A consultant specializing in equal opportunity issues is looking for a very different market. She needs to catch the eye of corporate chief executives and personnel vice presidents. Being quoted in The Wall Street Journal or Business Week would be ideal. The business section of the local newspaper where the consultant hopes to work (such as The New York Times, The Denver Post or The Los Angeles Times) is another outlet. Trade publicity could also be important. What industry does the consultant specialize in? What publications do the top brass of that industry read for their own business news? Those would be other publications where the consultant should seek publicity.

As you can see from these examples, bigger isn't necessarily better when it comes to targeting an audience. The major media such as Time, Newsweek or network television news may not be your best bet. The important factor in selecting the media where you would like publicity is not the size of the publication or news station, but its audience. Is that audience the group of people who are most likely to become your customers? For that reason, publicity in a weekly neighborhood newspaper may be as valuable to you as a story in a national magazine.

What's more, if you've correctly identified your audience and that of the medium you're approaching then you stand a good chance of getting coverage. After all, the media is seeking stories which are of interest to their audience, and if you have something to offer their segment of the market then they'll often be delighted to hear from you. People magazine must always focus on stories of national interest, but a gardening magazine has the luxury of being able to devote space to a very specific problem encountered by some gardeners. By the same token, a local publication can take far more interest in the lives and businesses of local residents than can any other type of media.

*

Contacting the media is discussed in great detail in the next section, but for the purpose of targeting your audience there's one rule-of-thumb I think you ought to know now: Stick with the media you know. It will save you time and effort. When you don't know the publication or the program, you can't be sure who the audience is. There's no sense in spending time trying to get publicity in a publication which isn't really right for you.

Of course, there is nothing wrong with doing some homework by reading a few different magazines or channel- or dial-switching for a few weeks to learn about different publications or programs. Just don't expect to get publicity from a particular outlet until you've taken the time to understand a bit about it.

WHAT DO YOU HAVE TO SAY?

Once you have an idea who your audience is, the next decision is what you want to say to them. <u>What do you want people to know about you?</u>

Perhaps you already have something specific in mind. You may want to announce a benefit, the opening of a new business, expansion of service, introduction of a new product, a staff promotion, an announcement of an award or the occurrence of a special event. If so, we'll be talking about the best way in which to announce such information later on in this section. However, most people I work with are in need of something more general. <u>They want press information explaining who they are.</u>

To serve this function, I recommend preparation of a <u>background press release.</u> It can be used to suggest feature stories, as a basis for interviews or to send along with other press announcements. Or the release itself can be converted slightly to announce something completely different. If you're establishing a complete publicity program for your business, the background press release will be your most <u>valuable tool</u>.

Finding a News Hook for a Background Press Release

Think about the different types of feature stories you see on television or read in the newspaper. Rarely is the story line simply, "how this person started a business." <u>There's almost always a twist to it</u>. Perhaps this person overcame great adversity to start a business, or perhaps the company is the first of its type in the community, or perhaps an organization performs a unique service for the city. These various angles of approaching the story are known as "news hooks."

A news hook or a news angle to the story is almost always essential when trying to get publicity, and it will add zest to your background press release. Members of the press are often so busy that they may not have time to think of the news angle themselves. If you are able to give them a "hook" and present them with interesting facts, then you'll be way ahead of the game in getting publicity.

Take a minute to consider what makes you, your business or your organization stand out. In all likelihood, there is something unique about who you are or the way your business or organization is operated. Is your business the first of its type in the community? Are you offering a more complete service than your competitors? Are you a native of the community who has returned because you like your hometown so much? Or has your club or organization discovered a new community need and dedicated itself to finding a specific solution?

For additional ideas, consider some of these possibilities:

* Plant shop has plant doctor who makes house calls.

* Restaurant features cooking by chef who has just recently retired from his post as chef at the Four Seasons in New York.

* Hardware store owned and managed by a woman.

* Bookstore specializes in special genre of book (only stocks mysteries or science fiction, etc.)

* Woman orthodontist specializes in orthodontia for adults.

* Puzzle company has specialty line of made-to-order puzzles.

* All-male cleaning company offers household service tailored to the needs of the working woman.

* Community service club devotes 75 percent of time and money to aid for needy families.

* Conservation group dedicates itself to preservation of local endangered species.

* Dance troupe specializes in modern choreography by local choreographer.

As you can see, each of the above could be developed into a full article about each particular business or organization.

The main element all these ideas have in common is that they tie into a current trend or fill a current need. For that reason, the news media might consider them to be of interest to their audience.

To explain more fully:

More and more women are returning to work, and they are often taking jobs in nontraditional areas for women. A woman hardware store owner fits into this trend as does the all-male cleaning team who may be needed to clean her home. The woman orthodontist story has two possible news angles: There are few women dentists, so she could be of interest from that point of view, or a story could focus on the current trend of the increasing number of adults who are having orthodontic work done for both cosmetic and health reasons.

The bookstore, the plant shop, the restaurant, the puzzle company and the dance troupe stories are of possible interest because they are offering something different to the public. Incidentally, the puzzle company may actually sell very few made-to-order puzzles, but the service may be worth offering for the news value. There's nothing wrong with adding something to your business or service simply as an attention-getter. However, anything changed or added for the sake of publicity

must be a <u>legitimate offer</u>--one you're prepared to back fully--
or the idea could backfire, and it would be senseless to run
that risk.

The community service club and the conservation group are
both performing public service functions of particular interest
to their local community. What's being done for needy families?
How does the club function? In conservation, what local
species are endangered, and what's being done to protect
them? Both of these subjects would be of interest to local
community residents.

At this point, I would like to stress that the <u>news angle</u>
for your background release <u>need not be earth-shattering.</u> Of
course, the more successful you are at coming up with a news hook
which ties into a current trend, the better it will be. However,
some stories just don't lend themselves to that. In this case,
your background press release should simply be written in as
interesting a manner as possible. The important thing is that it
should <u>clearly present the basic information about your company</u>
<u>or organization.</u>

(For sample background press releases, see pages 22 and 36 .)

If you'll turn to the special work sheet on page 25
you can begin to work out what your best news angle--
or angles--might be. Also, be sure to note down some of the more
interesting facts about your business or organization. This will
be helpful when you actually start writing your press release.

Keep in mind that <u>what you have to say may differ from</u>
<u>audience to audience.</u> For example, your hometown newspaper

would want to know immediately that you grew up there and are the son or daughter of a current resident.

Or if you've targeted a publication read by potential customers then your press release should make clear why that audience will be interested in you. What do you or your business have to offer this particular group of readers? Convenience? A unique product or service? Personalized attention to their needs?

When writing for your professional peers, the message may be the same as for your customers, but the language might be more technical. Or you might add a paragraph explaining the professional reasons you decided to offer a particular service or product. Is it to reinforce customer goodwill? Does the product or service have a particularly high profit margin? There are obviously many aspects of your organization that would be of special interest to people in related lines of work. Then, of course, it's up to you how much you would like to share with them.

If you're having trouble pinpointing what you would like to say in your press release, why not ask the opinions of friends and associates? Often they can quickly identify that unique quality you may simply take for granted.

Sample Background Press Release

The following will give you the general idea of the content of a background press release. Also see the press release on pages 36-37. (Book format dictates that these releases have been printed front-back, but note that press releases should always be printed on only one side of the page.)

(BACKGROUND RELEASE)

Contact: Sandy or Alan Lovell
The Cookie Loft
Kennebunkport, Maine
(207) 555-1111

FOR IMMEDIATE RELEASE

THE COOKIE LOFT IN KENNEBUNKPORT IS MAINE'S
FIRST SHOP CATERING EXCLUSIVELY TO COOKIE LOVERS

Kennebunkport--The Cooke Loft is the first shop in Maine which caters
exclusively to cookie lovers. The store, which specializes in cookies
made with all-natural ingredients, first opened in June of 1978 and
has enjoyed several very successful seasons in the resort town of
Kennebunkport.

The Cookie Loft company is the brainchild of a photographer and
dancer husband-wife team who wanted to test their ingenuity at something
potentially more lucrative than the arts. A cookie shop seemed like a good
idea to Sandy and Alan Lovell who noted the success of ice cream shops
and yogurt stores. Both had had experience working in restaurants, and
since baking was Alan's hobby, everything seemed right for starting a
retail cookie outlet.

(MORE)

COOKIE LOFT--page 2

Chocolate chip, peanut butter, mocha chip, sunflower coconut, carrot raisin, coconut oatmeal, lemon walnut, sweet potato and molasses crisp cookies are among the house specialties. "We make all our cookies from scratch with only the best of natural ingredients," says Alan. "These cookies are made with butter--not oleo, for example."

Getting the store started with no previous experience in the business required energy and dedication. Among the lessons to be learned quickly was how to convert a home recipe for 60 cookies into a commercial baking recipe for 500. And the first week they were in business was a particularly challenging time. The bowl for the industrial mixer had not arrived, so Alan hand-stirred all the batches of cookies!

Hard work has proven worthwhile for the Lovells. Within five weeks they had recovered their initial investment. And as time passes, the fame of the cookies grows. One day a family from Montreal arrived announcing that other Montreal residents had told them, "Be sure to stop at the Cookie Loft!" In another instance, a Boston woman who planned to do a lot of entertaining at her summer home in Maine carefully coordinated her driving time from Boston with Sandy Lovell in order to arrive in Kennebunkport just as the last of her 26 dozen cookies came out of the oven.

The Lovells have also owned and operated another Cookie Loft in York Beach and have recently established a year-round base in Portland. Now known as Alan's, the sandwich/ice cream/cookie shop is located at 15 Exchange Street. During the winter, the Cookie Loft cookies can be purchased there.

-0-

TRANSFORMING THE BACKGROUND RELEASE INTO A NEWS RELEASE

One of the important aspects of the background press release is that it can be altered slightly to convey different, more specific messages. Let's take another look at the Cookie Loft background release to see how it can be changed into a more news-oriented release.

Perhaps the Lovells decide they need to do a special promotion in order to increase business at the start of the new season. Their transformed release might begin as follows:

TWO-FOR-THE-PRICE-OF-ONE SALE TO BE OFFERED BY
COOKIE LOFT FOR FIRST WEEK OF NEW SEASON

Kennebunkport--In celebration of the company's fourth anniversary, the Cookie Loft is offering a two-for-the-price-of-one sale to all customers during the first week of the new season, June 6-12. The Cookie Loft is located in Kennebunkport and is a specialty shop catering exclusively to cookie lovers.

(The press release then picks up with the second paragraph of the original release.) ...

- - - - - - -

The more timely lead gives the Lovells a new reason to send out a press release which, of course, presents a new opportunity for potential press coverage. Obviously, if a newspaper has already done a feature on them, this new angle is not enough to merit another in-depth story. However, the new release may attract the attention of other media and would certainly merit a column mention in any tourist-oriented publications.

WORK SHEET FOR PLANNING YOUR PRESS RELEASE

Who are your customers (past, present and potential)? What other groups would you like to have know about your business (competitors, peers, civic leaders, etc.)?

What media are these people likely to read, watch or listen to?
(You will probably need to make a separate "media" list for each of the groups mentioned above.)

What do you want to tell them about yourself? To answer this, consider:
- -What makes your business different?
- -What are your business' strengths?
- -Why should a customer come to you rather than to your competitor(s)?

You may come up with more than one message you want to convey. If so, each can be developed into a separate press release which will give you more than one news angle with which to promote your business.

Chapter III

HOW TO WRITE A PRESS RELEASE

As we've discussed, the purpose of a press release is to inform the media of news which you hope will interest them. Because your release may receive only a few seconds consideration, presentation is very important.

The person to whom you're sending the release is likely to be a harried newspaper editor or a television assignment editor. They work under the constant pressure of deadlines. In order to sift through the mail and the incoming news possibilities, they need to be able to count on how information will be given to them.

That's where the format comes in. Press releases are designed to give a straightforward presentation of your story through a good, clear headline and a concise introductory paragraph telling who, what, when, where, why and how. The more quickly the editor can assess your story, the more likely he or she is to be interested in what you're offering.

THE FORMAT

As you'll see from the basic format that follows, a press release is simply designed and easy to read:

Contact: Name
           Company   ) SOURCE INFO
           Address
           Phone Number)

                            FOR IMMEDIATE RELEASE) RELEASE
                                                     DATE

SUMMARY HEADLINE TYPED IN CAPS   )
) HEADLINE
GIVING STRAIGHT FACTS OF STORY   )

Dateline--Press release follows in short, straightforward) BODY OF
paragraphs in the inverted pyramid style.   ) RELEASE

-0-

Source Information

"Source information" appears in the upper left corner.
This is nothing more than the name, address and phone number
of the person whom the media can contact if more information
is needed. In most situations, your own name or that of a
staff member will be appropriate.

If you are reproducing the press release on letterhead
stationery which contains the company name and address, then
name and phone number are all that are necessary. But even
if your phone number is printed on the letterhead, be sure to
put it with the source information anyway. That's where an
editor expects and wants to be able to find it. (And be sure
the phone number you include is one which is always covered
during business hours! An editor won't call more than once
or twice.)

The Release Date

Most press releases are labeled "FOR IMMEDIATE RELEASE." This means that the story can be used as soon as it is received or at the earliest convenience of the press.

If a release does not specify "FOR IMMEDIATE RELEASE," then it would specify a date: "FOR RELEASE, MONDAY, MARCH 26," for example. This is acceptable, but it can lessen your chances for coverage. By specifying a particular date, it means that the press must hold your release for a period of time. In general, the more complicated your news is to handle then the less interested in it they may be.

- - - - - - -

When Specifying a Date Might be Appropriate:

A community service awards dinner sponsored by a nonprofit organization might be an example of an occasion when sending a release with a specific date might be appropriate. In this case, the story would be of obvious interest to the community. Therefore, the local media would probably be interested in covering it.

Press material announcing the community service award winners would be prepared ahead of time. The information might then be labeled, "FOR RELEASE, SATURDAY, MARCH 10, 10 P.M."--the date and time the dinner should be over. Editors would then know that on the Saturday late evening television news or in the Sunday morning paper, they could report the names of those who had been honored at the dinner.

In this case, the system has advantages for both sides. The organization gets publicity for its dinner, and the editors have material in advance which they can count on using.

In special situations, specifying a particular release date and/or time can work to your advantage. But use it sparingly.

- - - - - - -

The Headline

The headline of the press release is a <u>straightforward summary of the main content</u> of the release. It is always typed in capital letters.

Catchy headlines are not appropriate on press releases, because what the editor expects is a factual summation telling him exactly what the story is.

When writing the headline, be sure to put the reader-interest information first: "FREE WORKSHOP ON ENERGY CONSERVATION FOR HOME OWNERS TO BE HELD..." rather than "MASON HARDWARE TO HOLD WORKSHOP..." In this case, the important information for the reader (and therefore, the editor) is <u>what</u> is happening and for <u>whom</u>, not who is sponsoring it.

The Dateline

The dateline is nothing more than <u>the city in which your press release originates.</u> "New York," "Denver," or "Albuquerque," for example--wherever your business is located. The dateline is particularly helpful when sending a release to newspapers or magazines which cover several different regions.

The Body of The Press Release

Since press information used to be primarily geared for the print media, press releases follow the format of newspaper stories. As you may remember from English class, news stories are always written in a form known as the <u>inverted pyramid</u>, giving all <u>vital details at the beginning of the story while other information is provided in descending order of importance</u>:

The Inverted Pyramid

WHO WHAT WHEN WHERE WHY HOW	< everything they <u>need</u> to know
IMPORTANT INFORMATION	< details you'd <u>like</u> them to know
MISC. INFO.	< good information but nothing vital

The reason for this structure is because news stories--and press releases--need to be of <u>flexible length.</u> If space permits, the whole story may run. Otherwise, only the first paragraph or so of a release may be used. If the story has been written in the inverted pyramid style, then the most important information will still be conveyed.

Though radio and television people do not need this format for the same reasons newspaper editors do, it is still a concise, easy-to-read method for presenting your information.

<u>THE WRITING STYLE</u>

You don't need to be a professional copywriter to tell your story in a press release. All you need to do is identify exactly what you want to say and adapt it to the format just given you. (Also read through the sample press releases to get a feel for writing up the material.) In addition, here are some general guidelines:

Keep your sentences and paragraphs short and your wording relatively simple.

Avoid glorifying your story. Try to be as objective as possible, and <u>let the merit of the story speak for itself.</u>

"Fantastic," "world's best" and "one-of-a-kind" are descriptions which have no place in a press release unless you have <u>facts</u> to back you up. If you're claiming to be the "first," then be sure you are. If your business is the "oldest" in the area, then provide a date to substantiate your claim.

Why such caution? There are two reasons. First, <u>a self-serving release won't sell well to an editor.</u> It's better to pique her curiosity with a factual press release, so that she'll send a reporter out to cover your story. (Let <u>them</u> say you're wonderful!)

The other reason for not glorifying your own story is because editors sometimes need copy they can quickly plug into a blank space on the page. They often take a story and print it word-for-word from the release. If your release gives a glowing description of your business, then a newspaper editor--who, of course, strives to fill the paper with objective reporting-- can't select your release to fill that blank space. She probably won't have time to send a reporter out to see if you're as good as you say you are.

But suppose you do have good news to report---there are ways to include positive information about yourself. If you have statistics or facts which tell the story, use them. If your sales volume has increased 50 percent since starting a new promotion, then that's a story. Or if a regular customer gears his schedule to coincide with when you receive shipment of a certain product, then that situation can be described. (You do not even need to mention the customer by name.)

You can also place such information in quotes. Perhaps the customer who plans his schedule around shipment of that certain product would be willing to be quoted as to how great it is.

You can also quote yourself on subjects such as expansion of service or increase in traffic. As long as the release is written so that it does not appear that the newspaper or magazine is saying all those wonderful things about you, then your good news can be useful news to the media.

Finally, your press release should conclude with a paragraph indicating what you want the reader, listener or viewer to do as a result of reading or hearing about your story. "Call for more information: 555-5555," "Tickets can be purchased at the door" or "Call 555-9999 for reservations" are examples. The editor has the right to include this information or not. Since it may be cut, format dictates that the information belongs at the end. Remember, you're not paying for ad space--you're asking for free exposure. The editor will decide what is appropriate for his publication or program.

TYPING IT UP

Your press release should be <u>neatly typed and double-spaced with wide margins</u> for easy reading. Be sure to proof it for typing or spelling errors. Editors want to sense professionalism behind the releases they select for possible stories.

If your release runs more than one page, then spacing should be planned so that you have a paragraph ending at the bottom of any page, and a new paragraph beginning at the top of the next page.

"(MORE)" should be written at the bottom of each page which leads on to a continuing page of the release. Then subsequent pages should be labeled with a release title and page number in the upper left corner: "STORE OPENING--Page ___"

On the last page, indicate the end of the release by putting "-0-" or "###" or "END" after the final paragraph.

<u>Press releases which run more than one page should always be stapled</u>. This minimizes the chance of a page of your release being lost.

REPRODUCING YOUR RELEASE

If you've ever seen press releases sent out by major corporations, then you're probably aware that large companies

often have special letterhead printed up for their press
releases. "News" or "Press Information" is often emblazoned
across the top of the paper in bright colors, and the release
may be printed on colored stock. Of course, the purpose of
the lively appearance is to attract attention.

How--on a limited budget--do you compete with this?
You don't need to. Time after time, editors have told me that
it is the content--not the letterhead--which ultimately
sells the story.

However, most editors also note that a neat, attractive
presentation never hurts. This does not mean that you should
spend large sums of money on presentation, but it would be a
good idea to give some thought as to how you can present
your release attractively using the business materials at
hand.

Most of you have doubtlessly taken time to select
letterhead stationery for your business. (More on this subject
in "Your Image.") If so, then sending your press release
out on your regular letterhead is probably the most attractive,
distinctive method for presenting your material. How you
go about doing this largely depends on the number of copies of
the release you'll need.

For Fewer than 10 or 15 Copies:

If you need only a few copies of a release, I would seriously
consider having each copy individually typed on your letterhead stationery.

The exception to this would be if your letterhead happens to

be black printing on white stationery. In this case, you can
simply type the release on the letterhead and photocopy that
original to make multiple copies of the release. (Why can't
you do this with all letterhead? Because if you have colored
stationery or a multi-colored logo, the letterhead usually doesn't
photocopy well. And remember, you want your release to attract
favorable attention. Sending a badly reproduced release will
get your publicity campaign off on the wrong foot.)

Never send carbon copies. They smudge easily and are
difficult to read.

For 15 Copies or More

Offset printing is an excellent way of reproducing your
releases, because the appearance will be so good. A "quick
copy" printer can print your release on your own letterhead
efficiently and economically. Though you will generally have
to order copies in quantities of 100 or more, the expense is
still small. In the New York area, you can get 100 copies of
a one-page release printed on letterhead stationery for
about $5. (One printer I've found will also photocopy releases
onto letterhead for 5¢ a copy. The appearance isn't quite as
good as offset, of course, but if you only need 25 copies or
so this would be a good alternative to ask about.)

When pricing printers, be sure to mention that you will be
providing your own letterhead paper. This can make a
difference in cost. Then once you find a printer whose prices
seem reasonable, try to establish a working relationship.
Printers can often make excellent suggestions concerning
appearance and ways to cut costs.

SENDING IT OUT

Your press release should be mailed in a neatly typed
business-size envelope, preferably addressed to a specific
person at the publication or broadcast station. (This will
be covered fully in "The Media.")

SUMMARY GUIDELINES FOR WRITING A PRESS RELEASE

* Souce information (name, address and phone number) appears
  in the upper left corner.

* The release date--typed in capital letters--appears slightly
  below the source information on the opposite (right) side of
  the page.

* The headline summarizes the content of the release and is
  typed in capital letters. Be sure to lead with the reader-
  interest information: "FREE WORKSHOP ON ENERGY CONSERVATION..,"
  not: "MASON HARDWARE TO HOLD WORKSHOP..."

* The first paragraph of the release answers: who, what, when,
  where, why and how. The inverted pyramid style is used
  for the remainder of the release.

* Paragraphs and sentences are short and to the point. Glowing
  descriptions are to be avoided.

* When typing the release, always double-space and leave wide margins.

* Any release should be carefully proofed for typing or spelling
  errors. Remember, you're asking for free editorial space,
  so it's important that your release make a good impression.

* If a release is more than one page long, spacing is planned
  so that one paragraph ends at the bottom of a page, and a
  new paragraph begins at the top of the next page.

* "(MORE)" is typed at the bottom of any page which leads on
  to a continuing page of the release. A title and page number
  ("STORE OPENING, Page ___") identifies any subsequent pages.

* On the last page, the end of the release is indicated by
  "-0-" or "###" or "END" after the final paragraph.

* For any release running more than one page, all pages should
  be stapled together to keep them from getting separated.

* Always send a good, clean copy of a release to the media.
  Never send a carbon.

* The release should be mailed in a neatly addressed business-
  size envelope and should usually be sent to a specific
  person.

Sample Background Press Release

The following release demonstrates all the elements of
the format just discussed.

(BACKGROUND RELEASE)

Contact: Joan Dorman Davis
College Admission Counselors
6133 Brooklyn Avenue N.E.
Seattle, Washington 98115
(206) 522-6900

) *SOURCE INFO*

FOR IMMEDIATE RELEASE) *RELEASE DATE*

COUNSELING FOR THE COLLEGE-BOUND OFFERED) *HEADLINE CAPSULIZES STORY*
BY NEW BUSINESS IN THE SEATTLE AREA

Seattle--Joan Davis is the Northwest's first freelance college counselor.
A former Assistant Dean of Admission at Amherst College, Ms. Davis now
runs College Admission Counselors, a private service which provides
information and counseling for the college-bound.

) *BASIC FACTS*

"Many people need help in selecting the right college," says Joan
Davis. "Today students can choose from a wide variety of schools, but
they need to keep in mind what environment will really be best for them.
College Admission Counselors is an independent agent--a matchmaker, if you
will--whose purpose is to bring the right students and the right
colleges together.

) *IMPORTANT DETAILS*

"Too many college freshmen realize too late that they have enrolled
in the wrong place. They haven't taken time to consider the many options
they have," she continues. "With a few hours of counseling and some
informed inquiry about various schools they can make their college experience
more challenging, interesting and rewarding. Why should anyone spend
time dragging themselves through the wrong college?"

(MORE)

COLLEGE-BOUND COUNSELING--page 2

When meeting with a student Ms. Davis reviews transcripts, available
test scores and recent written work. Clients are also asked to bring a list
of their extracurricular activities. The talk leads to a discussion of the
most desirable--and affordable--educational environment for the student.

While her clients are primarily high school seniors and transfer
students, Ms. Davis also meets with returning students (those who have
been out a year or more and wish to resume thier studies.)   She helps
clients with testing, financial aid, application essays and interviews.

"My purpose is to provide a special, much-needed resource for the
college-bound," says Ms. Davis. "High school guidance counselors do
their best, but they haven't visited college campuses all over the country
and can't be expected to keep abreast of annual changes in admissions poli-
cies, curriculum and financial aid at over 1,000 private colleges. It makes
sense to see a professional college counselor if you want to make an
informed decision regarding college choice."

Fees for College Admission Counselors are $100 for the basic service:
a two-hour meeting, a written evaluation of each student's personal options
and a list of appropriate colleges. For an additional $150 students benefit
from follow-up phone calls and an additional meeting with Ms. Dorman; they
also receive an informed letter of recommendation to the colleges of their
choice as well as a subscription to her newsletter for the college-bound.

College Admission Counselors is located at 6133 Brooklyn Avenue, N.E.,
Seattle, Washington 98115. For more information call Joan Davis at
(206) 522-6900.

IMPORTANT DETAILS

SUPPLEMENTARY INFORMATION

WHO TO CONTACT

HOW TO WORK WITH A WRITER: FOR THOSE WHO PREFER ADDITIONAL HELP

Before continuing, I'd like to take a minute to stress how very important it is that you take the time to put together the best press release you can. After all, good press coverage should increase business and heighten your image within the community. Since the press release has to do your talking for you, it's vital that it be a good one.

The information provided in this section tells you all that you need to know to write your own material. However, if you're among those who get writer's block at the very thought of having to put your thoughts down on paper, then I strongly recommend that you hire a freelance writer, a moonlighting reporter or a P.R. or advertising copy writer to prepare a basic release. Even a college student who is willing to spend a few minutes studying this section of The Publicity Manual might write a good press release for you.

If you decide to hire a writer, be prepared to pay approximately $12-20 an hour or more. (This rate will vary according to your area of the country and the experience of the writer you select.) If you are well-organized and can provide the writer with specific information as to what you want said, then most writers could do a satisfactory job for you in about 4-5 hours. (If you have filled out the work sheet at the end of "The Basics," it will provide a writer with much of what you want to say.)

To find a writer, try calling local newspapers, magazines or public relations or advertising agencies to see if someone might

be willing to do a little part-time work for you. You might
also watch the classified ads in local papers and magazines to
see if anyone advertises their services. If a college student
seems better suited to your needs, the career placement offices of
most universities have free job posting services so that students
can contact you about any work you might have for them.

If for some reason you're hesitant to work with a writer on
an hourly basis, you may prefer to agree on a flat rate. At
city prices, approximately $150 should buy one good press
release. If you want additional material written up from the
same background material, then each additional piece might cost
another $60 or so. Of course, if an additional press item
requires more research then you should expect the cost to be
a little higher. (The prices here are rough estimates of the
cost of hiring a freelancer or moonlighter. Agency prices for
written work would be much higher.)

Spending money for good written material can be a shrewd
move for business owners. You're paying a one-time charge for
material that can be used over and over, and if you're not
comfortable writing your own material, then it saves you the
time you would have to spend preparing it.

- - - - - - - - - - -

Chapter IV

HOW TO TAKE ADVANTAGE OF PUBLICITY OPPORTUNITIES

One of the best ways to get publicity on a consistent basis is to make news out of what's happening anyway. Sending out press material on a new product or an added service, formally announcing staff promotions or making a news event out of an annual street festival you participate in are just some of the publicity possibilities readily available to you. In this chapter we will take a close look at how to take advantage of the following:

- Product or service news

- Special events

- Company news

- Business observations transformed into news (the "news that's under your nose")

- "Timely" news

- Your viewpoint as news: letters to the editor

HOW TO ANNOUNCE NEWS OF A PRODUCT OR SERVICE

In the last few years, there has been tremendous growth in the amount of newspaper and magazine editorial space given to products and services which would be helpful to readers. This means good news for those seeking publicity! Many publications now have "new and useful" columns, and there are also entire sections in many newspapers--going by various names such as "Home," "Living," "You" and "Lifestyle"--which devote entire articles to various products and services. And the one thing you can be assured of is that they are constantly looking for new things to write about.

But again, the challenge is left to you. There are many companies vying for that free editorial space, so your product or service news release must clearly tell an editor why your information would be of interest to that publication's readers. It's up to you to decide what is newsworthy about the product or service you wish to publicize.

Suppose you own a kitchen gadgets store, and you'd like to publicize a new battery-powered whisk which has just come in. In determining a news angle, some of the things to consider are: Why is a battery-powered whisk better than the old-fashioned arm-powered whisk? Is it the latest in kitchen gadgets being used by famous chefs? Is this the first time it has been available in your community? Or is it the perfect Mother's Day or Valentine's Day gift?

The press often likes to tie this type of news in with special holidays, so linking your product or service news to an upcoming holiday may give you an edge on the competition. (More about this when we discuss "Timely" news on pages 79-84.)

Product publicity sometimes fares better if you can provide a photograph of the item. Major magazines and newspapers usually prefer that their own photographer take the actual shot that runs with a story, but a photograph you send in with the release can often attract favorable attention. (For more information on photographs, see pages 103-112.)

If you're in a service business, then you may want to write a release announcing expansion of your services and/or reminding the public of services you already offer.

A tutorial service specializing in helping elementary school children with reading difficulties may have discovered that math is an equally big stumbling block for certain youngsters. To announce the expansion of their services to cover tutorial help in math, the tutorial service's release could describe how they identified the problems the children seemed to encounter with numbers and what the service could do to help. Of course, a short paragraph describing the reading assistance already offered would provide the opportunity to get publicity for both aspects of the tutorial program.

It may seem relatively easy to explain the public's need for a new service or product, but don't forget that <u>there will always be new ways to look at old items</u>, too. For example, if thermostats are kept at a lower temperature in winter, consumers are going to be eager to know about all the old ways for keeping warm. There should be room for publicity on long underwear, good woolens, flannel sheets and flannel nightgowns. <u>Current events can give a new publicity twist to items that have been around for years</u>.

The same holds for service publicity. If high unemployment is in the news, then this is a perfect time for releases about the services of employment agencies, temp services and career counselors.

Sample Product and Service Press Releases

The content of the release is nothing more than a straightforward story about the most newsworthy aspect of the product or service. The format follows that of the releases we have already studied.

Contact: Jane Valdez
           Heatco Industries
           410 West 32nd Street
           New York, N.Y. 10001

           (212) 555-6578

FOR IMMEDIATE RELEASE

NEW PORTABLE ELECTRIC HEATER, "BIG-10" USES

10% LESS ELECTRICITY AND DELIVERS 10% MORE HEAT

New York--Heatco Industries announces a breakthrough for their portable heater line. The new technology of Heatco's "Big-10" heater allows it to use less electricity to deliver more heat.

Three years of design, development and testing by Heatco engineers led to the unique energy-saving process. By using specially treated copper and tungsten coils which heat faster and retain the temperature longer, the "Big-10" units use 10 percent less electricity and deliver 10 percent more heat. (The percentage claims are a result of independent laboratory testing--the study is available upon request.)

Louis Kroll, President of Heatco, noted the significance of the product when making the announcement: "Now, more than ever, we need energy-efficient equipment to help keep us warm yet save energy costs. We believe the technology represented here is a breakthrough for the heating industry. It will help both consumers and producers in their efforts to save energy."

The "Big-10" heaters will be sold through major hardware and retail stores.

-0-

Contact: Mark Wilson
          Wilson's Dry Goods
          2923 High Street
          Miami Beach, Florida 33140

          (305) 555-8812

FOR IMMEDIATE RELEASE

"HOT CUP" NOW AVAILABLE

EXCLUSIVELY FROM WILSON'S DRY GOODS

Miami Beach--Wilson's Dry Goods has secured an exclusive distribution

supply in the Miami area for the Go-Anywhere Hot Cup, a portable

coffee maker and hot water heater manufactured by Travelset.

The Hot Cup has caused quite a stir with local customers who

saw national advertising for the product but were not able to find the

item locally. Due to an unusually heavy demand, there had not been

enough Cups shipped to fill all requests. Wilson's Dry Goods has

now received a special shipment of 250 Hot Cups, so the item is now

available.

Mark Wilson, store owner, says the demand has not subsided, and

if he sells all 250 Cups, he will again be accepting orders. There will be

no increase in price. Hot Cups sell for $23.95.

Wilson's Dry Goods is located at 2923 High Street in Miami Beach.

The phone number is 555-8812.

-0-

(NEW SERVICE)

Contact: Meg Jones
           The Office Center
           115 West 10th Street
           Portland, Oregon 97201

           (503) 555-8642

                                    FOR IMMEDIATE RELEASE

NEW EXECUTIVE SHOPPING SERVICE--DESIGNED TO SAVE TIME

FOR BUSY EXECUTIVES--BEGINS AT THE OFFICE CENTER

Portland--An Executive Shopping Service, designed to save time for busy
executives, is now being offered by The Office Center.

"Shopping can be very time-consuming," says Meg Jones, Manager of
the Executive Shopping Service and former merchandise manager for Flatt's
Gift Shop. "Most executives can't spare the time to shop, and some have trouble
deciding on the right gift for the right person. Our service provides
consultation, leg work, a recommendation and the final purchase. In other
words, we take care of everything from planning to wrapping and delivery."

Ms. Jones will consult with clients on the type of gift, the occasion
and the price range. After that, a search is made for the right selection.
A final check with the client guarantees satisfaction.

Charges for the service are 25 percent over the gift price, with a
minimum gift order of $35. There is a one-time registration fee of $10.
Once a client is registered, the Executive Shopping Service will keep track
of birthdays, anniversaries, holidays and special occasions and provide
reminders and gift suggestions well in advance of any special date.

The Office Center, located at 115 West 10th Street, is Portland's
one-stop business resource for office space, secretarial help, printing
and messenger service. Phone Meg Jones at 555-8642 for more information
on the Executive Shopping Service.

-0-

HOW TO PLAN AND ANNOUNCE SPECIAL EVENTS

Sponsoring a special event can sometimes serve several useful purposes. It generally promotes goodwill within the neighborhood or community, builds visibility for your business or organization and provides the opportunity for possible publicity.

However, I must enter some words of caution here. Staging a special event can be costly, and the publicity results are never guaranteed. There are no "sure bets" in publicity. When you're trying to get coverage of an event being held on a special day at a special time, it makes it all the more difficult to predict how much news coverage you might receive. In fact, many special events get no post-event coverage at all.

When I was doing publicity for a new restaurant in midtown Manhattan, we planned a street festival as a special promotion. An entire midtown street was closed to traffic for two hours one lunchtime in June. Several notable jazz musicians provided entertainment, and free food and soft drinks were dispensed by the restaurant staff. Judging by the size of the crowds, one would view our event as an unequivocal success, yet we got very little post-event press coverage.

Why? Because at the same time Muhammad Ali was appearing at another outdoor event near Madison Square Garden. When editors were faced with deciding whether a street festival or Muhammad Ali was more newsworthy, the heavyweight champ won. And there's no way to prevent something like that from happening. If it hadn't been Muhammad Ali it might have been a three-alarm fire which commanded the attention of the print reporters and TV crews. All in all, we did view our street festival as a success. We had succeeded in attracting the attention of potential customers--workers whose offices were located near the restaurant. Though we would have liked post-event publicity, we still had accomplished our primary goal.

As long as you go into it with your eyes open to the fact that there may or may not be media coverage, there are many very good reasons for staging a special event. If--like the street festival--you can sponsor an event which will be attended by or attract the attention of potential customers with or without media coverage, then a special event can be a very successful type of promotion. If you should get media coverage, then all the better.

The type of special event you choose must, of course, be in keeping with the nature of your business. An executive search firm would be out of place at a street festival and quite at home holding an open house, for example. When selecting the type of event you might like to sponsor, here are some things to know about various types of events:

Sponsoring an Event for Charity or Performing a Public Service

This could be anything from donating and dedicating trees to the city to having a Christmas party for the local orphanage. Because these are noncommercial events, the press seems to feel somewhat more comfortable about covering them.

One particular benefit of staging an event for the public good is that you are genuinely doing something of service, and with or without press coverage you will be promoting goodwill for yourself and your company.

Another thing to keep in mind is that there may well be a backdoor approach to getting publicity. Many nonprofit or community organizations have newsletters or belong to national associations which have magazines or newsletters. By performing a public service for one of these organizations, you may be able to be written up in their bulletin or newsletter.

For example, suppose you do sponsor a Christmas party for a local church-operated orphanage. News of the orphanage is almost surely reported in the church bulletin, so your Christmas party should certainly be mentioned. You might even provide them with a photograph of the party for use in the bulletin.

With this approach, you can receive excellent publicity for your company. You may not have landed the daily newspaper, but you will have publicity in a publication where the readership may be equally valuable to you. You've shown that you care about something that members of that church care about, too. They will think highly of you for that.

Guest or Celebrity Appearances

Guest or celebrity appearances are terrific when they work well, but they can be dangerous. What if no one shows up to meet your "celebrity?" Of course, if your celebrity is Sophia Loren who is in town to promote her book, then that should be no problem. But it's difficult to predict what kind of a "draw" a lesser celebrity will be.

Local television and sports celebrities can draw a good crowd, but I would try to sound out how popular a person really is before scheduling anything. Even then, you should arrange for a certain number of friends to drop by just in case the crowd is light.

Ceremonies And Open Houses

Ceremonies and open houses are other types of events which can be held. Generally, the people who attend these events are invited by special invitation. If you are having an open house, then you'll doubtless be sending invitations to business associates and customers. If you do want and get pre-publicity inviting the public, then that's fine, but your open house will be a success with or without it.

The same holds true for ceremonies. If an occasion is worth marking with a special ceremony, then there will surely be certain VIPs who will attend. Again, if the public should come, all the better, but you're not depending on them for the turnout.

Street Festivals

Street festivals or fairs are another type of event to sponsor. Of course, the success of a festival depends on the <u>cooperation of a good number of merchants</u>. With or without press coverage, a festival usually <u>generates goodwill, builds visibility for the participants and may boost sales for the day</u>.

Press coverage of these events is difficult to predict. In New York, there are many street fairs which never receive coverage, yet the Ninth Avenue Food Festival often gets nationwide television exposure. There are a couple of probable reasons for this: First, Ninth Avenue is usually curb-to-curb with people which makes a very good visual shot for television. And since most of the network news programs originate from New York, it's a story that the news personnel are very aware of.

Workshops, Clinics and Drop-In Sessions for the Public

When well-conceived, these types of special events stand an excellent chance of accomplishing what they were intended to. One appliance store was so pleased with its successful series of free audio equipment workshops for women that they promptly scheduled a series of air conditioning workshops to discuss such topics as methods of choosing the right unit for your home, how to judge energy efficiency and what minor repairs can be done by the owner at no cost.

This seems an excellent example of a special event planned and executed wisely. However, it's important to understand that <u>media coverage would not have been a major goal</u>. Though the store obtained some additional visibility through pre-event publicity (notification that the event would take place), there wouldn't have been much hope for later press coverage--an air conditioning workshop isn't exactly a hot story. However, the store did accomplish two other important goals: they <u>achieved customer goodwill</u> by sponsoring a free event, and they <u>broadened their market potential</u> by educating the public. If unknowledgeable about what to look for in audio equipment, for example, a potential customer may get frustrated and decide to do without making the purchase.

Brokerage houses have long used free workshops run by brokers as a way to educate potential investors and make them feel more comfortable with the idea of investing.

Many other types of businesses can benefit as well. An electronics store might like to hold workshops to introduce people to home computers. Until consumers feel comfortable with the new machinery, they aren't going to buy it. A children's bookstore may be able to build traffic by sponsoring a regular Sunday afternoon story hour. A nonprofit organization dedicated to helping women re-enter the work force may have success with a Monday morning coffee hour and/or resumé clinic for unemployed women. And an interior decorator who sponsors a free workshop may be able to build visibility while educating potential clients as to how a decorator can be used to help save them both time and money.

Like the air conditioning workshop, these events stand a good chance of pre-event publicity and little chance of post-event publicity. However, if planned for the proper purpose, businesses and organizations can build visibility among their market base by scheduling these types of special events.

Even when the event is free, advance registration for the specially scheduled workshops would be a good idea. That way

you can prepare for the right size of crowd, or if the event
has not attracted enough attention you can cancel or re-schedule
for another time. Also, in your pre-event press release, you
may want to specify that there is no obligation to buy.

Auctions, contests, art exhibits and fashion shows are just
a few of the other types of special events you might want to
consider.

If you are inclined to try a special event, here are some
guidelines for increasing the success of the event and your
chances of media coverage:

The Time Schedule

If media coverage is important to you, then the hour for
which you schedule the event can be important: Is it a convenient time for news people?

One small breakfast promotion I planned received excellent
television coverage. I feel sure that part of the reason
they came was simply that there wasn't much else happening at
8 a.m., and this particular station happened to have a crew
available then.

Does the hour for which your event is scheduled allow enough time
for the press to make their deadlines? Television is your
main concern here--their staffs are generally trying to make a
5 or 6 p.m. deadline for the early evening news, while print
journalists would have a bit more leeway for the next day's
paper. In addition, a print reporter may write the story from
a general, human interest standpoint so that the story could
run several days after the event. Television tends to want
to report an event as it happens, so they are more concerned
with scheduling a story into reportage of that day's happenings.

In general, if you would like to be covered by the early
evening television news, you should schedule your event for
early in the day--any time up until about 3 o'clock should be
a relatively good time. If the nature of your event dictates

that it should be held in the evening, you may still have a
shot at the late evening news. Stations may not have as many
staff people available for assignments as they do during the
day, but you should certainly send them press material anyway.

"But what about the on-the-scene coverage stations do for
some events?" you may be thinking. You're right, they do
sometimes provide live coverage. Now that more television
stations are using minicameras and remote broadcast equipment,
they are broadcasting more events live during the news. But
that is a complex type of coverage generally reserved for
special types of news stories. For the most part, you'll be
far safer scheduling your event earlier in the day or hoping
that a crew will cover it for the late evening news.

As for scheduling events on holidays or weekends, there are
both pros and cons to this. On the plus side, these tend to
be quiet news days, and the press is often looking for interesting
stories to cover. However, your competition can be tough. For
example, on a holiday your community may have one or two events
which are held annually. Those tend to be the events that
receive news coverage rather than a new promotional event
with which the media is unfamiliar.

Another factor for concern when scheduling an event for
a weekend--particularly Sunday--or a holiday is that
stations are often operating with a skeleton staff. There
may not be personnel available to cover your story.

But when it gets right down to it, the best advice I can give
you for choosing a good time is to call your local station
(The best time to call is usually early morning before the
reality of their daily deadline is upon them.), and ask
their advice. Make it clear that all you want is their
opinion--you are not trying to get a commitment for coverage.
If your event needs to be on a weekend, then you can ask if
Saturday might be better than Sunday. And what time is best
for holding your type of event? Of course, there is still the
risk that they won't be able to cover it, but at least you
will have given it your best shot.

Timeliness

If you can <u>tie an event into the season or the time of year</u> you may also increase your chances of coverage. In late March when everyone's mind is on taxes, a bookstore might arrange for the author of a tax preparation guide to be on hand to answer questions.

In the spring, a garden shop owner might give away small packets of seeds and have a gardening expert demonstrate different types of planting that can be done at that time of year.

"Test-Marketing" Your Idea

Even with proper timing and timeliness, there are still no guarantees with a special event. To better evaluate the potential success of your idea, <u>observe what others are doing and see if it works.</u>

Along with my good experiences, I've had my disasters. The breakfast promotion I mentioned earlier which got good press coverage was a real failure at bringing in the people. To promote the idea of business breakfasts in our hotel restaurant, I had suggested and planned a series of five breakfast meetings with speakers scheduled to speak on various financial topics. Four of the mornings we had barely a dozen people. The fifth day the topic was women and money, and about forty women attended---the turnout we had hoped for all five mornings.

Had I looked around at what else was happening in New York, I would have seen that women seem much more interested in seminars than men. There was a good reason why no one else was scheduling such events for men---they weren't going to come. Most of them get the investment advice they want directly from their broker.

From this experience, I learned how important is is to <u>"test-market" an event before scheduling it.</u> Obviously, you can't really test out an idea before planning it, but you can observe what other people in the community are doing. <u>Note how they promote their events</u> (newspaper advertising, fliers, publicity,

etc.) Then check on what their response was. See what events
draw well. Topics concerning women and careers or women and
money seem to bring crowds right now, for example. And parents
will generally take their children to a puppet show or a story-
telling session. Observe what is working in your community,
and then re-evaluate whether your event has real potential
for success.

Pre-Event Publicity (Notification That an Event Will Take Place)

For papers or magazines with "events" columns, sending a
release to the "events" editor will usually get your event
listed. (Timing the arrival of your release is important
so call the publications to find out what their deadlines are.)

Some publications also run short articles about upcoming
events. Study your local media. If they do, call to find
out to whom to send the material. Charity or community service
events as well as ceremonies have a good chance of coverage as
local news, so those releases should definitely be sent.

Will pre-event publicity bring in a crowd? That's difficult to say. It depends on the publication as well as the
type of coverage. (A feature article will bring more people
than an "events" listing, for example.) You can research
this by talking to others who have had events listed in the
various publications, or if yours is an event where reservations are requested, you'll be able to get an idea of
the response ahead of time.

When a special event works well, it can be a very successful
type of promotion, but careful planning and adequate research
are a must beforehand!

Sample Special Event Press Releases   (See the following pages)

In reading through the releases, you might note the following
about these particular promotions:

Release #1 (students visiting printing plant): Note that
Woburn's motive for this event is not solely for publicity.
He is having trouble finding young people interested in
learning the printing business, and he hopes this promotion
will increase interest in the field. Wisely, he is also
taking advantage of the opportunity for media exposure.

Woburn has a good chance of getting local coverage because
he's performing a service which will be of interest to the
community.

Release #2 (marathon champ to appear at Sam's Sporting Goods):
By scheduling this event for a Saturday afternoon, Sam has
reduced the risk of not having a crowd. That's doubtless a
busy time for the mall, so there should be a good flow of people
throughout the afternoon.

A shopper newspaper might put this in their "events"
listings or even run a short blurb about it, but it is doubt-
ful whether this publicity will increase Sam's crowd very
much. (His celebrity is not that noteworthy.) However, the
activity will attract interest which should build the store's
visibility within the mall.

Release #3 (yogurt-tasting contest): This type of release might
get picked up by a local weekly newspaper or by a campus paper.
But again, the restaurant doesn't need publicity to find contest
participants. If the only contestants are people who come by
the restaurant for a meal that day, it won't affect the success
of the promotion. It's a fun idea that people should enjoy,
and the Health Haven will be promoting goodwill.

A reporter looking beyond the event might see that there's
a feature story to do about the merits of yogurt. If the
idea for the story springs from having received this release,
then he or she would surely contact Steve Freed for more
information.

Release #4 and #5 (library ceremony and realtor open house):
As discussed earlier, both these organizations might like to
have the public attend events such as these, but they won't
be relying on public attendance to produce the needed crowds.
    Both releases have a good chance of being printed locally,
because both concern issues which would be of interest to
their respective communities. But note that the opening of
the real estate office would not be particularly newsworthy
if it wasn't located in a new urban renewal district.

Release #6 (street festival): Since a street festival takes the
cooperation of so many people, more expensive methods of notifying
the public can be employed. Fliers, banner and posters can
all be used to help build excitement for the event.
    This release might make an "events" listing column in a
local newspaper or magazine, but the primary point of this
festival will be to build neighborhood goodwill and increase
the visibility of the individual merchants.

Release #7 (workshop): This event should work well as a joint
promotion for The Little Boutique and Marian Blake. They
stand a good chance of getting pre-event publicity. The
new store will benefit from the additional visibility, and Ms.
Blake will be able to broaden her market base by having the
opportunity to explain her services to potential clients.

Contact: Vernon Woburn
          Woburn Press, Inc.
          1130 Canal Street
          Virginia Beach, Virginia 23600
          (804) 555-7098

FOR IMMEDIATE RELEASE

HIGH SCHOOL STUDENTS TO VISIT PRINTING PLANT

DURING SPECIAL "JOB OPPORTUNITIES" DAYS

Virginia Beach--On Tuesday, January 8, tenth grade students in the city and
county high schools will visit Woburn Press, a working printing plant, to learn
more about various businesses and future job opportunities as part of a six-week
"Job Opportunities" series. At Woburn Press, students will go on a tour of
the plant and hear brief talks about some of the jobs available in the
printing industry.

The "Job Opportunities" program is part of a new working relationship
between local businesspeople and educators. Vernon Woburn, owner of Woburn
Press, was instrumental in putting the program together. Finding that
recruitment and training of new employees is becoming increasingly difficult,
Woburn met with other business owners and eventually the newly formed
committee proposed the "Job Opportunities" program to the School Board.

"We expect that the project will benefit both students and the Virginia
Beach business community," says Woburn. "Students will be more knowledgeable
about vocational opportunities, and local businesspeople may have a larger
pool of applicants to draw from as more information is learned about the
various businesses."

Smith Shipping, One-Stop Mart, Essex Finance, Rockco Industries and
Greenleaf Publishers are also participating in the program. Other interested
business owners should contact Vernon Woburn at 555-7098.

-0-

Contact: Sam Smith
          Sam's Sporting Goods
          West Lake Mall
          Bergenfield, New Jersey 07422

          (201) 555-3184

FOR IMMEDIATE RELEASE

MARATHON CHAMPION TO APPEAR AT SAM'S SPORTING GOODS

Bergenfield--Hank Reese, winner of the 1979 New Jersey Marathon, will be at
Sam's Sporting Goods in the West Lake Mall at 2 p.m. on Saturday,
August 4.

   Reese, who has also won the Smithtown Marathon, the Cross-Country
Championship and numerous other race titles, will be giving jogging tips
and answering questions about running and physical conditioning. His
highly regarded 15-minute film on proper warm-up for runners will also
be shown several times throughout the afternoon.

   A complete line of running shoes, outerwear and books and
training guides will be on sale at Sam's throughout the week.

   Sam's Sporting Goods is located in the northeast corner of the
West Lake Mall in Bergenfield. For more information call (201) 555-3184.

<u>(SPECIAL EVENT)</u>

Contact: Steve Freed
          Health Haven
          640 Garfield
          Fort Collins, Colorado 80524
          (303) 555-8810

FOR IMMEDIATE RELEASE

YOGURT-TASTING CONTEST TO BE HELD AT

HEALTH HAVEN ON SATURDAY, NOVEMBER 17

Fort Collins--Frothy Vanilla, Peachtree Delight, Boisterous Boysenberry and
Pretentious Pistachio are just a few of the exotic flavors that will be sampled
and identified in the first-of-its-kind Yogurt-Tasting Contest on Saturday,
November 17 at Health Haven, 640 Garfield in Fort Collins.

Anyone can participate simply by coming to the restaurant between noon
and 4 p.m. Each participant will be given three sample flavors to taste and
identify from the collection of 25 yogurt dishes available at Health Haven.
Those who successfully identify all three flavors will be given their choice
of any three quarts of yogurt free.

Steve Freed, owner of Health Haven, developed the contest to introduce
more people to one of his favorite foods: "Yogurt offers something for everyone. Its flavors, its consistency and its nutritional value make it the
perfect food for today's active people."

Health Haven restaurant offers a menu of health food from soup to nuts.
Started in 1977 in a small store-front location, it has increased in size and
popularity with the addition of a take-out service and a specialized luncheon
menu for office workers and busy professionals. Sandwiches and salads-to-go
are part of the special, customized service. The yogurt flavors are the specialty
of the house, with Steve Freed himself concocting new flavors each month.

-0-

Contact: Mary Smith
          Wheelersburg Library
          200 Linden Avenue
          Wheelersburg, Ohio 43810

          (614) 555-3854

FOR IMMEDIATE RELEASE

CLINTON LIBRARY ASSOCIATION MARKS 50TH ANNIVERSARY

ON DECEMBER 4--SPECIAL CEREMONY PLANNED

Wheelersburg--Wheelersburg's Clinton Library Association will celebrate its
50th anniversary on Tuesday, December 4. A special ceremony will be held at
the Wheelersburg Library at 10 a.m. to commemorate the occasion.

The Clinton Library Association was formed in 1932 to support local
library activities in the Wheelersburg area. Started with an endowment from
the Henry C. Clinton Fund, the group has maintained a long tradition of
library service and support both with volunteer manpower and funding.
Among the services it provides are reading hours for children, a special
nature hike program, hospital library services and volunteers and a library
scholarship program for the study of library sciences.

State Library Commissioner Alice Withers will present the Association
with a special anniversary plaque which will hang in the Main Reading Room.
The ceremony will be attended by local and state library representatives as
well as officials from the Wheelersburg municipal government. The public
is invited to attend.

The Wheelersburg Library is located at 200 Linden. Call 555-3854
for additional information.

-0-

Contact: Jane Jones
           Smith Realtors
           333 Vine Street
           Watertown, North Carolina   27681
           (919) 555-2323

FOR IMMEDIATE RELEASE

TOURS OF URBAN RENEWAL AREA AND OPEN HOUSE JUNE 8
TO MARK OPENING OF SMITH REALTORS' BRANCH OFFICE

Watertown--The opening of Smith Realtors' new branch office at 310 Main Street
heralds the migration of suburban companies to the urban renewal district
of downtown Watertown. An open house and tours of the area will be held at
the new location on Friday, June 8 from 2-5 p.m. The public is invited to
attend.

     Mayor Irma Rogers will introduce the featured speaker, Councilwoman
Mary Williams, who conceived and developed the urban renewal project.
Ms. Williams will outline the next steps for revitalization of the downtown
area in a brief talk scheduled to begin at 3 p.m.

     Following the ceremony, small tour groups will be leaving from the Smith
office to view the six-block area where the urban renewal project is
nearing completion.

(MORE)

SMITH REALTORS' OPENING--page 2

Smith Realtors is the first among many businesses who are

supporting the city's revitalization efforts by moving back downtown.

"As a company involved in planning and developing real estate,

Smith Realtors is delighted to be among the group which will be

re-establishing a business district in downtown Watertown," says

Clark Gandoff, President of Smith Realtors. "Looking to the future,

no city is going to be able to afford to let its center deteriorate, and

I'm proud that Watertown is providing for the future now."

For more information on the open house and tours, please

contact Jane Jones at 555-2323.

-0-

(SPECIAL EVENT:
STREET FESTIVAL)

Contact: Gloria Dillon
          Dillon's Meats
          33 Market Place
          Sacramento, California 95813
          (916) 555-7435

FOR IMMEDIATE RELEASE

THIRD ANNUAL MARKET PLACE STREET FESTIVAL

TO BE HELD ON SATURDAY, MAY 10

Sacramento--The third annual Market Place Street Festival will be held on Saturday, May 10 from 11 a.m. to 6 p.m. Market Place merchants will sponsor special activities and offer sample delicacies, and a Dixieland band will provide entertainment. Market Place will become the domain of pedestrians for the day as the street will be closed to traffic during festival time.

The Market Place Merchants Association has again received 100 percent participation in the festival, and the result is a wide variety of offerings for the day. The Coffee Mill is recreating a Viennese cafe just outside their shop where coffee and pastries will be served. A puppet show for the children is being sponsored by The Captain's Ship. Performances are scheduled for 11 a.m. and 1, 3, and 5 p.m. Dillon's Meats will be serving finger sandwiches made from their newly developed recipe for barbecued chicken.

The ferris wheel, a highlight of last year's festival, will be brought in for the children's pleasure again this year. Proceeds from ticket sales for the ride will go to benefit the local ASPCA.

Additional information about the Market Place Street Festival may be obtained by stopping by any Market Place merchant to pick up a flier.

-0-

(SPECIAL EVENT: WORKSHOP)

Contact: Ruth Levine
         The Little Boutique
         2031 Green Street
         Lexington, Kentucky 40502

         (606) 555-2111

                          FOR IMMEDIATE RELEASE

FREE FASHION-IMAGE WORKSHOP FOR BUSINESSWOMEN

TO BE HELD AT THE LITTLE BOUTIQUE, SEPTEMBER 30

Lexington--A free fashion-image workshop for businesswomen will be held

on Tuesday, September 30 at 5:30 p.m. at The Little Boutique, 2031 Green Street.

The workshop will be conducted by Marian Blake, an image consultant.

    The workshop will begin with a brief fashion show to demonstrate a

variety of attractive executive styles, and then such topics as no-fuss

make-up for the executive woman and fashions that travel well will be

discussed. Time will also be devoted to questions from the audience regarding

personal image in order that Ms. Blake can address topics of specific

concern to those present.

    As an image consultant, Ms. Blake's specialty is personal service

for the executive woman. From initial wardrobe analysis and lifestyle

discussion through to the search for the "right items at the right price,"

Ms. Blake has helped many executive women sharpen their business image.

She formerly worked at Bowman's Department Store as a fashion consultant.

    Fashions for the style show will be provided by The Little Boutique,

a new woman's store in Lexington devoted to high quality clothing at

affordable prices. The Little Boutique is owned by Ruth Levine.

    Advance reservations are requested. Phone The Little Boutique at

555-2111. No purchase is necessary to attend.

                                  -0-

HOW TO MAKE THE MOST OF COMPANY NEWS

Anniversaries, company financial news, awards, staff promotions, new employees and company participation in the community are occurrences which are taking place within your organization all year round. They are also a never-ending resource for your publicity efforts. <u>A simple release citing specific happenings within the company can make news out of news which is happening anyway</u>.

Company Business News

If you've had a strong year financially, won a special award or elected a new board of directors, then <u>you have good press information for the business pages of your local papers</u>. Though many newspapers focus almost entirely on the national financial news, almost all will also have a regular columnist or reporter who covers the local business happenings.

If you live in a small- to medium-size community, then you might like to <u>phone this reporter directly</u> to ask what type of information he particularly likes to receive. (Some newspapers do an annual edition featuring complete news on local businesses, so you might also inquire about that.) You should then plan to <u>keep him abreast of the major business happenings within your organization</u>. If you develop a good working relationship with the reporter, you may eventually be able to simply call in your story. Otherwise, follow the regular press release format to announce your business news.

If your local newspaper is <u>The New York Times</u>, <u>The Los Angeles Times</u> or any other major metropolitan daily, then your outlook for this type of newspaper coverage is not particularly favorable. However, if you have especially good news to report, sending a release can never hurt.

However, there are other avenues to pursue. <u>Trade publications</u> within your industry may also print

business news. Women business owners might also investigate
some of the business-oriented women's magazines and newsletters.
They sometimes cover this sort of information, and if so,
you would do well to send them a release.

News of Employees

Publicizing staff promotions or the hiring of new employees
can be a good way of making your company more visible while
expressing to the staff members that you're proud to have them
as part of your team.

Trade publications usually make a big effort to report changes
in staff. All you need to do is furnish the information. Most
run a one-sentence blurb about each person, and some will print
photographs if you have one available to send along.

Some local newspapers may also give space to such announcements.
Watch the paper for a few days to see if this type of news is
being covered.

In cities, the larger metropolitan newspapers often don't
have space for anything but major business announcements.
However, if your staff member lives in a neighboring community
or in the suburbs, there may be another opportunity for coverage.
If his or her community has a local newspaper--even a weekly
one--send the announcement to them. Generally, the local media
is delighted to run news of their residents. (Be sure that
the press release you send them mentions that the person is
a local resident, or mention it in an accompanying note.)

Community Involvement

The importance of community involvement will be discussed
in "Your Image," but for now, keep in mind that any activities
you or your staff members participate in may be of news value.

If you or a staff member have been appointed to a special
committee of a service club or if you've been asked to serve on
the board of directors of the Chamber of Commerce, the Rotary
Club or the Association of Women Business Owners, that's reason

for announcement. Most local newspapers (again, with the exception of the major city newspapers) try to cover such news. This type of publicity not only gets your name across, but it spreads a very positive message about you and your company's involvement in the community.

Anniversaries

Small- and medium-sized newspapers, tourist-oriented pub- lications and trade magazines will sometimes run a short article or column mention of news of a company anniversary.

But an anniversary also gives you the opportunity for trying again for possible feature coverage. You can write up a special release for the occasion or simply re-write the first paragraph of your background release and send it off to newspapers and magazines or radio and television stations whom you think might find your business of interest.

Sample Company News Press Releases (See the following pages)

In reading through the sample release, you might note the following:

Release #1 (corporation announces record earnings): Because Citlon stock is available on the Pacific Stock Exchange and can be purchased by investors nationwide, this release should be distributed nationally. Besides mailing to The Wall Street Journal, Business Week, AP, UPI and the Tucson papers, Citlon would be well-advised to use a distribution service to mail to a computerized mailing list of business editors nationwide. (For a reasonable fee, a distribution service will mail your release to the type of editor and publication you specify. This can be useful for large, nationwide mailings of press material. See "Resources" for additional information.)

Because Citlon's news is particularly good this year, they might also mail the release to local and regional brokerage houses to remind them to spread the word about the stock.

Release #2 (announcement of a design award) This news would be
of interest to most Montana newspapers and should be guaranteed
coverage in the Great Falls paper. Others who might pick up
the story would be any arts-oriented newsletters or magazines
published within Montana.

Release #3 and #4 (new manager named and business owner appointed
to mayor's council): These releases would be of local interest
and should also be picked up by the trade publications of their
respective industries.

Release #5 and #6 (anniversary announcements): Both the companies
sending out anniversary announcements should study their local
publications to see where this sort of information might be run.
There may be room for it with local business news, or perhaps
it should be sent to the reporter covering other types of
local happenings. As discussed earlier, the releases might
also spur interest for a possible feature story if sent to
the right reporter. (If Larry Key hopes for feature coverage,
he should probably send along a background release--possibly
focusing on his home maintenance clinics--as his anniversary
release is really not detailed enough to attract feature
interest.)

(BUSINESS NEWS:
FINANCIAL REPORT)

Contact: Max Stephens or Madeline Cox
          Citlon Corporation
          457 Third Avenue
          Tucson, Arizona

          (602) 555-3280

FOR IMMEDIATE RELEASE

CITLON CORPORATION ANNOUNCES

RECORD EARNINGS FOR 1981

Tucson--Citlon Corporation, a hardware products manufacturing company, announced record earnings of 29¢ per share for 1981 vs. 12¢ per share for 1980. The announcement was made at the company's annual meeting held February 1, 1982. Net income rose to $303,800 for the year vs. $134,000 for 1980.   Sales for 1981 reached record levels of $1,952,600.

In making the announcement, Larry Sanderson, President of Citlon, noted that the strong demand in home hardware products and hand tools had helped push sales and profits to their record levels. "Based on the outlook for 1982, our predictions are for another strong year for the company," he said.

Citlon is listed on the Pacific Stock Exchange.

-0-

Contact: Chris Allen
          Hillside Crafts
          2218 Court Street
          Great Falls, Montana 59403

          (406) 555-9395

FOR IMMEDIATE RELEASE

HILLSIDE CRAFTS COMPANY WINS DESIGN AWARD

Great Falls--Hillside Crafts, the Great Falls-based tile design company,
has been honored with the 1979 MDC Design Award from the Montana Design
Council.

Chris Allen, designer for Hillside Crafts, was given the award for
the "inspiration and enthusiasm" reflected in the Hillside designs. The
award, a silver plaque, was presented at the annual Design Council
luncheon in Billings on October 31.

The last Great Falls resident to win the award was textile designer
Marie Voss who won it in 1973. She now enjoys a national reputation for
her work.

It was the first award for the 27-year-old designer whose shop
is located at 2218 Court.

-0-

(STAFF PROMOTION)

Contact: John Brown
          Home Bakery, Inc.
          200 West 4th Street
          Pueblo, Colorado 81003

          (303) 555-5438

                              FOR IMMEDIATE RELEASE

ROY STEVENS NAMED MANAGER OF HOME BAKERY, INC.

Pueblo--Roy Stevens has been named Manager of Home Bakery, Inc., it was
announced today by Ben Park, President of the company.

    Home Bakery is the baker and distributor of Mrs. Flynn's Cheesecake,
her famous Crumb Cake and a host of other specialty dessert and cookie
items sold under the Home Bakery name.

    Mr. Stevens joined the company in 1976 as plant supervisor where
he instituted major changes in the company's baking and packing systems.
In his new role as manager, he will oversee all plant operations and
distribution for the entire Home Bakery company.

    Mr. Stevens is a graduate of Colorado State University where he
majored in business administration. After a four-year term with the
U.S. Navy, he returned to Pueblo and joined Home Bakery, Inc.

    Stevens enjoys growing vegetables in his garden and skiing on
the local slopes. He is married to Sally Donovan Stevens, who is also
a native of Pueblo. They have three children.

                              -0-

Contact: Joan Lewis
          Better Furniture, Inc.
          1011 Main Street
          Comstock, Michigan 49433

          (616) 555-9436

                                        FOR IMMEDIATE RELEASE

PETER STANLEY NAMED TO

MAYOR'S ADVISORY COUNCIL ON BUSINESS

Comstock--Peter Stanley, President of Better Furniture, Inc. of Comstock,

has been appointed to the Mayor's Advisory Council on Business.

     The Council is made up of local business and community leaders who

will advise the mayor and the city government on ways to improve and

attract more business.

     Stanley moved to Comstock in 1966 from Lansing where he grew up.

After working as a buyer for furniture in Ferrill's Department Store for

six years, he launched his own business in 1972.

     Stanley also serves on boards with Park Hill Hospital and with

the Chamber of Commerce.

     His other civic activities include Rotary Club, the United Fund

and coaching the Little League.

     Stanley and his wife, Margaret, live on Mill Road with their

two children.

                                -0-

(ANNIVERSARY)

Contact: Larry Key
          Key Hardware
          310 Silver Street
          Albuquerque, New Mexico 87103

          (505) 555-9239

                                    FOR IMMEDIATE RELEASE

KEY HARDWARE MARKS TENTH ANNIVERSARY
THE WEEK OF SEPTEMBER 15

Albuquerque--Key Hardware is celebrating its tenth anniversary during
the week of September 15 with special promotions and activities.

     Now an Albuquerque fixture known for its Saturday fix-it clinics,
the hardware and houseware supply store will offer special discounts on
store merchandise throughout the week.

     Larry Key, owner of the store, credits much of the success of his
business to the local community interest in home maintenance: "People
here realize that fixing a leaky faucet or patching a wood chip doesn't
call for a master craftsman. I can provide them with all the materials
they need, and our clinics will furnish the know-how."

     Key Hardware was founded in 1969 by Larry's father, Bob Key.
Bob is now retired and Larry and his brother, Steve, manage and operate
the business. The main store is located at 310 Silver and there is a
branch store located in the North Street Mall.

                                    -0-

Contact: Donna Stone
          The Sandpiper Restaurant
          333 Brock Street
          East Beach, Massachusetts

          (617) 555-4321

                                        FOR IMMEDIATE RELEASE

THE SANDPIPER RESTAURANT CELEBRATES

FIFTH ANNIVERSARY ON MONDAY, OCTOBER 15

East Beach--The Sandpiper Restaurant, known for its fresh crab and lobster

specialties, celebrates its fifth anniversary on Monday, October 15.

     What started as a sideline for Donna Stone and her sister, Joanne, has

grown into a fulltime thriving enterprise. Their specialty menu--featuring

20 different lobster dishes--and their fresh approach to local seafood

bring patrons from as far as Boston to the Brock Street establishment.

     During the first year of operation, Donna Stone also taught at Milford

High School while Joanne worked part-time as a bookkeeper. By 1975 the

Sandpiper following had grown to the point that Donna felt she could leave

teaching to oversee the restaurant operation fulltime. A year later,

Joanne also left her other job to devote more time to the Sandpiper.

     "The wisest move we ever made was spending the money to hire the

best chef we could. We were serving scrumptious dishes right from the

start, and those who came told their friends about us," says Donna.

"I would say that's the one main reason our investment paid off."

     The Sandpiper, located at 333 Brock Street, is open 7 days a week

for lunch and dinner. Call 555-4321 for reservations.

                                   -0-

HOW TO GET PUBLICITY FROM NEWS THAT'S UNDER YOUR NOSE

What personal qualities make a good chief executive officer? What toys are selling well this Christmas? What over-the-counter medical items are of increasing interest to consumers? What have psychologists at the local university learned about fear? Surely you've seen articles on topics such as these.

They are excellent examples of how companies can make the most out of information that is available to them anyway--the news that is under their noses. For example, the story about the best personal qualities for a CEO relied heavily on data provided by an executive search firm. These figures may have come from information the search firm compiles on candidates routinely, or perhaps the company sent out a special questionnaire--a process simplified by the fact that they automatically have an up-to-date mailing list from their regular files. Either way, the information was relatively easy for the executive search firm to assemble, because it was material they deal with all the time anyway.

An article in a Colorado newspaper noted that local pharmacists had observed an increase in sales of self-help medical kits like blood pressure-measuring devices. It took no more research for the pharmacists than simply noticing that customers seemed to be requesting these items more frequently. They then backed their observations with a comparison of yearly sales figures.

In both these cases, the companies are doing nothing more than reporting a trend they have observed and providing data to substantiate their observations. You can do it, too, by looking around you--there's news in the news that's under your nose.

What's more, the "trend" story you can create for free is a type of publicity which gets enough media coverage that some companies spend large sums of money just to develop this sort of story. Cigarette companies, long frustrated by the ruling which forbids them to advertise on television, are constantly looking for ways to keep their product in the public eye, and Virginia Slims has turned to the trend story for part of their exposure. Every few years they commission a polling company to do an extensive Women's Opinion Poll covering topics such as why women work and the future of the family, etc. The findings are then released by Virginia Slims, and the media coverage is always excellent.

Not only does coverage of trend stories tend to be good, but this type of publicity is particularly helpful for several other reasons: It gives you another reason to approach the press; it provides you with a very strong news hook for your release; and it helps establish you as an authority in your field by making you appear thoughtful and knowledgeable--a very favorable light to be seen in when trying to increase business.

How To Gather The Material

To see how the material can be gathered, let's look at some examples:

The proprietor of a roommate matching agency may have noted that instead of solely seeing a young clientele, she was seeing many elderly people as well. To back up her observation, it would take no more than a few minutes of going through her files to determine what percentage of her clients were older. Then either a glance at some of the client questionnaires or phone calls to some of the older people who have sought roommates would lend insight into the reason for the trend.

In another example, a hardware store owner may have noticed an increase in the number of women buying material to do their own home-repair projects. (Statistics on this might be available from the national association if a study of the ratio of male-to-female hardware store customers has ever been done.) But even if no statistics are available, it's a perfectly valid observation to make---it's what one store owner has observed in one particular community. Without statistics, you would just be careful not to make any broad generalizations. The observation could then be substantiated by checking with a few women customers, quoting them by name or not according to their preference. Their answers would probably tie in with other national trends. For example, if they were to be asked why they are doing more of their own home maintenance, their answers might be the following: a)Too expensive to hire someone (ties in with inflation); b) They are single or divorced and there's no one to do it for them (follows trend of the increasing numbers of female heads of household); c) They have recently learned the skills to do their own work (relates to the increase in adult education courses teaching women new skills).

Other types of observations companies could make might include a bookstore that noticed an increase in demand for all astrology books, perhaps as a result of a recent best seller or a movie or TV show on the subject. A restaurant, bar or liquor store might observe a change in drinking habits. Or a plant store may spot a trend toward a certain type of plant, while a pet store notes that the sale of hamsters has dropped off in recent years.

Also, keep in mind that the facts and statistics don't have to be yours. The government as well as many other types of organizations release facts and statistics on all sorts of subjects all the time-- from the unemployment rate to the number of women business owners to how many people obtain advanced degrees. If you come across statistics which pertain to your business, you can <u>cite those statistics and relate them to your own observations or to what the statistics may mean on a local basis</u>. (See the second of the sample press releases, page 78.)

Once you have selected the subject, you can write your press release. The first sentence should clearly state the trend you have observed while the remaining paragraphs go on to substantiate the claim. <u>Be sure to include some general information about your company or send along a background release</u>.

<u>Sample Press Releases Concerning Trends</u> (See the following pages)

Release #1 (more tourists going to Africa): This release features information which was probably easily accessible to Travel Associates as the statistics are based on their non-business trip volume for two different years. This is material they probably follow closely anyway for marketing reasons. The information in the last paragraph could have come from a questionnai routinely conducted by those who organize the safaris. Note that the press release limits the observation to the travel habits of residents of St. Louis, but ties in with the global trend of the increasing number of species in danger of extinction.

Release #2 (increase in women MBA's): This release is a good example of a company which has taken statistics gathered by another organization (in this case, the National Center for Education Statistics which is part of the U.S. Department of Health Education and Welfare) and has related them to the company's own experiences. This release might spawn an article about Stern and his company, or it might inspire a reporter to do a broader piece about women MBA's, using Stern as one of the sources, naturally.

(BUSINESS TREND)

Contact: Jan Witkin or Anne Thompson
           Travel Associates
           3440 Delmar
           St. Louis, Missouri 63101

           (314) 555-8820

FOR IMMEDIATE RELEASE

ST. LOUIS TOURISTS GOING TO AFRICA

IN INCREASING NUMBERS TO VIEW ENDANGERED SPECIES

St. Louis--With more wild animal species facing extinction each year, travel
interest in African tours and safaris is becoming increasingly popular with
St. Louis tourists, according to data collected by Travel Associates of
St. Louis.

A check of Travel Associates' total non-business trip volume for
1978 and 1979 indicates a 30 percent increase in African tours and safaris.
The majority of the travelers spend 21 days touring the game preserves and
wildlife refuges of Kenya and Central Africa in organized air/land tours.

Despite high inflation and the decline of the dollar overseas,
American interest in African travel seems to represent a desire on the
part of many Americans to see what may be the last of wild animals in
their natural habitat.

Most of the travelers go in couples, either husband and wife or friends
traveling together. Both professional and amateur photographers are
especially interested in the special opportunities these trips offer.
Guides report that 95 percent of the travelers bring cameras.

-0-

Contact: Hank Stern
          Stern Associates
          101 Walnut
          Philadelphia, Pennsylvania 19101
          (215) 555-0978

                              FOR IMMEDIATE RELEASE

INCREASE IN WOMEN MBAS BRINGS MORE FEMALES

TO THE ATTENTION OF UPPER MANAGEMENT

Philadelphia--In 1971 the proportion of women graduates getting a masters

degree in business administration was only 4 percent. Today that percentage

has more than tripled, and certain schools report that up to 45 percent

of their current enrollment is female.

     "The trend of more women obtaining MBA degrees has facilitated our

progress in satisfying corporate demand for women with management potential,"

says Hank Stern, President of Stern Associates, executive recruiting

consultants. "We're placing three times as many women today as we did

ten years ago.

     "The women who go on to business school are proving they take their

careers seriously," continues Stern. "It indicates they are willing to make

a long-term commitment to the working world. Women also seem to gain more

from it than just business knowledge. Those who go on for the advanced

degree seem to feel more secure about where they are going. They have more

confidence. The bottom line is that an MBA generally makes a woman a very

attractive candidate for most corporations."

     According to Stern Associates, the woman who goes on to get her MBA

can have $5-15,000 difference in starting salary over what she would have

made with just a bachelors degree.

                              -0-

HOW TO MAXIMIZE YOUR NEWS BY BEING "TIMELY"

From a publicity standpoint, the fact that May 5th is Nelly Bly's birthday or that November 9th is the anniversary of the East Coast blackout or that July 11 is National Cheer Up the Sad and Lonely Day or that one week in January is designated as Don't Owe a Letter Week may be very significant to you.

Anniversaries of major events and days or weeks established to commemorate certain causes are a publicity seeker's dream. If you can tie your business in with one of these occasions, then you will likely have a good chance for additional press coverage.

The media recognizes many of these special occasions and is usually looking for stories that tie in with them. For example, in February on Good Morning America, an inventor was interviewed one Monday morning because over the weekend the nation had "celebrated" National Inventors Day. That same morning they talked to doctors about heart disease because February is Heart Month. Later that month on a different network on a different type of program, Captain Kangaroo had a special feature on his show which tied in with Save Your Vision Week.

The news media needs reams and reams of material in order to fill their air time or their pages, but one of the challenges left to you is to provide them with a reason why a particular story is news. These specially designated days give them an incentive to do certain types of interviews at various times of the year, and the story comes off seeming current and newsworthy.

To find dates which might be useful for your business, try consulting an almanac to see what you find. You can also obtain

a complete listing of dates in <u>Chases' Calendar of Annual Events</u>
which is published each year. (Available by mail order for
$9.95 from Apple Tree Press, Box 1012, Flint, Michigan 48501.) Many
of these occasions are sponsored by national associations intent
on furthering a cause. For example, National Safety on the Streets
Week in late October is sponsored by the National Safety Council. So
you can also <u>contact organizations</u> which relate to your business to
see if they recognize any special dates of interest to you.

Once you've chosen a date, a good way to tie in with it
effectively is to <u>offer the media helpful feature material</u> on
the subject:

An optometrist might mail out a press release with tips
for guarding against eyestrain in honor of Save Your Vision
Week. In October there is a National Pet Health Week, so a
veterinarian or pet store owner might write a release concerning
proper pet care. Also in October there is a National Jogging
Day, so a sports store owner might provide information on
proper warm-up exercises or even sponsor a marathon to mark the
occasion. Libraries usually do an excellent job of taking
advantage of National Library Week by sponsoring reading-related
activities. One week in June is designated National Be Silly
Week, and I leave that to your imagination.

On a more serious note, another part of being "timely" is
taking advantage of the news that comes your way. For example,
I happened to be teaching an ongoing publicity workshop during
the New York City transit strike, and a massage therapist was
among those in attendance. After observing the television news
which was emphasizing self-help ways of getting to and from work
and more self-help remedies for recovering from same, the therapist

asked what I thought of her sending out a press release on foot and leg massage techniques people could perform on themselves after a long day of walking, jogging or biking to work. Her idea couldn't have been better--she had observed what was happening in today's news and then tried to determine how she and her business could tie in with it.

Another good example of this is the opportunity which presented itself to local and national offices of the Multiple Sclerosis Society when Iranian hostage Richard Queen was diagnosed as suffering from MS. Though the media doubtless contacted many MS offices for more information once that news was revealed, it was also an opportunity for some aggressive work on the part of MS chapters. Press information being sent out should have answered questions such as these: What is MS? How is it treated? What is the likely prognosis for someone like Queen? Could any of the other hostages have caught it from him? What can the public do to help? Perhaps local victims of MS--many of whom are leading perfectly normal lives--would even be willing to be interviewed about how they deal with the disease. And of course, through this visibility and the additional public awarness of the disease, one would hope that the coffers for helping to search for a cure for MS would be greatly increased.

Like the releases concerning trends which we just discussed, this type of press release can lead to an extremely beneficial type of publicity because it increases the visibility of your business or organization and further establishes you as an authority.

Sample "Timely" Press Releases (See the following pages)

Both of these sample releases offer excellent feature material for either the print or broadcast media. Note that the second release is not based on commemoration of a specific day or week. Career Changers Ltd. is simply making news of the fact that many people change jobs in September--the release is still very timely.

("TIMELY" NEWS)

Contact: Cheryl Jackson
           My Best Baby
           2311 South Drive
           New Orleans, Louisiana 70140

           (504) 555-6908

                                    FOR IMMEDIATE RELEASE

ADVICE FOR NEW MOTHERS OFFERED

DURING NATIONAL BABY WEEK, APRIL 21-28

New Orleans--There comes a time when every new mother asks herself:

"Am I doing the right thing?" "Is this really what my baby is asking for?"

     To mark National Baby Week which runs from April 21-28 this year,

My Best Baby, a clothing store specializing in the needs of infants,

is offering tips on a multitude of subjects. Among them are a few

pointers on a baby's cry:

     -The tone of the cry is what to listen for. Crying is a baby's only

      way of saying he needs you, and the tone tells you how great his distress.

     -When a baby is allowed to cry for a long time, he can become so

      exhausted that it will be difficult for him to sleep even after

      you've seen to his needs.

     -But don't go running _every_ time your baby cries. Soon he'll be

      crying more frequently--sometimes just to have company.

     These and 100 additional tips for new mothers are in a brochure being

distributed by My Best Baby during National Baby Week. Customers will also

receive a discount slip for 10 percent off any future purchase.

     My Best Baby specializes in clothing needs for the newborn to the

3-year-old. All layette needs can also be found here. My Best Baby is

located at 2311 South Drive and is open from 10-6 Monday through Saturday.

Phone 555-6908 for more information.

                              -0-

Contact: Diana Foster
           Career Changers Ltd.
           810 Gilbert Street
           Houston, Texas 77098

           (713) 555-5168

FOR IMMEDIATE RELEASE

JOB HUNTERS ABOUND IN SEPTEMBER---

CONSULTANT OFFERS CAREER ADVICE

Houston--September is a big month for changing jobs. Executive recruiters
and personnel agencies note that following summer vacations, people
tend to start looking for that new job they've been wanting. Corporate
personnel departments report that September always brings an increase in
applications for new jobs as well as for transfers in corporations.

If you're considering a job switch in the coming weeks, career
consultant Diana Foster, who runs Career Changers Ltd, has some advice:

-Start by examining your own job. What do you like about it? What

do you dislike? This will help you identify the type of new job

you'd like to have.

-Your resumé should be neatly typed and should be written specifically

for the kind of job you will be applying for. Try asking yourself:

If you were the employer, what would you want to know?

-Since jobs usually come through friends and contacts--not through ads

or personnel agencies--let as many people as you can know you're looking.

-On the interview, dress in the image of the job you want and present

yourself in a positive manner.

-Above all, keep at your job search! Try doing one thing each day in

order to avoid getting bogged down and discouraged.

Career Changers Ltd. offers complete job-hunting assistance privately
and in groups. Call 555-5168 for additional information.

-0-

YOUR VIEWPOINT AS NEWS: LETTERS TO THE EDITOR

A sometimes overlooked opportunity for exposure is the "Letters To The Editor" column in newspapers and magazines. This is a good forum for nonprofit organizations, citizens groups and business owners who want to take a stand on an issue.

If you're a merchant who will be affected by a city council decision concerning urban renewal, then you may wish to express your viewpoint in a letter to your local newspaper. If you're a lawyer who has just read a magazine article which you think gives a misleading impression about some aspect of the law, then you may wish to respond to the article in a letter. If you're the chairman of the Parents for Better Schools Committee, then a letter to the newspaper editor is a good way of explaining what your group is trying to accomplish for the community and what other citizens can do to help.

The "Letters To The Editor" space is also a good way to achieve publicity in a publication which has eluded you. For example, a New York-based computer company had been eager to achieve exposure in Business Week and finally did so by commenting on a computer-related issue which had been raised in a previous issue of the magazine. Their viewpoint--and company name--was printed in "Letters To The Editor."

You can also use the column as a last-chance effort to benefit from an article in which you would have liked to have been included. One career counselor was disappointed not to have been interviewed for a job-hunting article which appeared in Redbook. After reading the article, she prepared a "Letters

To The Editor" piece offering some suggestions which were not mentioned in the article. Her letter was printed, gaining her the desired exposure in Redbook.

Not all letters to the editor can or will be printed, so the best way to get the feel for what is used is by reading the letters printed in the publications which would be of interest to you.

Keep in mind that though a newspaper or magazine will print divergent viewpoints, they will steer away from the inaccurate and from letters with an obvious commercial "plug" in them. In other words, a dry cleaner can't very well write about what a great job he does cleaning the clothes of local residents and expect it to run as a letter to the editor. Also, keep in mind that lengthy letters may have to be shortened, but that the editor will always try to maintain the overall tone and content of what you've written.

You should also remember that what you write will reflect strongly on your image. Take time to be sure you're comfortable with the viewpoint you express--you don't want to regret a letter written in haste.

When you have something appropriate to say about an issue or an event, this type of exposure can be a very valuable form of publicity.

Chapter V

OTHER TYPES OF PRESS MATERIAL

Though the press release is certainly the most common--and most useful--form of written material used in approaching the press, there are several other formats you should know about because they can be time-savers.

The tip sheet is a shorthand method for announcing a forthcoming event. It's simple to prepare and easy for the press to assess.

The biography press release is discussed in detail. Some of you will want one, and others won't need it. However, if you determine that it's a piece you'd like to have on hand, do it right after you finish your background press release. Then it will be ready when you need it.

Cover letters can range from a note written in longhand to a rather lengthy explanation of why your business or organization would be of interest to a particular audience. The letter format is often useful and can frequently save you the trouble of preparing separate press releases for various media.

The chapter concludes with a discussion of the press kit which is nothing more than a compact system for presenting your material to the press.

THE TIP SHEET

Another commonly used form of press information is the
tip sheet. <u>It is excellent for announcing a specific occasion
or event.</u> The format is as follows:

```
Contact:  Name
          Company
          Address

          Phone Number

                                    FOR IMMEDIATE RELEASE


                 SUMMARY HEADLINE


EVENT:

DATE/TIME:

LOCATION:

ADDITIONAL
  INFORMATION:
  (or
    "NOTES:")

                       -O-
```

A main advantage to this format is that an <u>editor can tell
at a glance what the event is and whether it suits his schedule.</u>

The tip sheet is a particularly good format for press
information being sent to <u>radio and television stations or
"events" editors</u> who simply need to know the basic facts about
what is taking place.

<u>Sample Tip Sheets</u> (See following pages)

The basic format of the sample tip sheets seems self-explanatory. Observe that the "Notes" or "Additional Information" section is used for giving additional details such as price information or telling a little more about the event itself.

Tip Sheet #1 (author to give talk on Valentine's Day): Several elements we have discussed throughout "The Basics" are made use of here. First, the event scheduled ties in nicely with a holiday. Since radio and television may try to do some sort of holiday coverage, they might well choose this event. Newspapers, for the most part, will want to run any Valentine's story on the morning of the 14th (prior to when this event will take place), but they might still run notice of the plans for the event, or they might even phone the bookstore to see if an interview with Mary Todd could be conducted ahead of time.

Also, note that the program for the next week is mentioned at the end of the tip sheet. This accomplishes two things. It establishes the lunchtime events as an ongoing program--not just a gimmick dreamed up for one day. It also gives a reporter or editor who finds do-it-yourself car repair particularly fascinating the opportunity to mark his or her calendar for next week.

Tip Sheet #2 (workshop about financial careers): This tip sheet will fare best with "events" editors. The workshop topic is not really new or different enough at this point to attract radio, television or newspaper feature coverage.

Contact: Jean Park
           Browsers Bookstore
           312 Main Street
           Northampton, Massachusetts 01060

           (413) 555-9239

                        FOR IMMEDIATE RELEASE

             AUTHOR OF THE RETURN OF HEARTS AND FLOWERS

                TO GIVE TALK AT BROWSERS BOOKSTORE

                         ON VALENTINE'S DAY

EVENT: Mary Todd, author of The Return of Hearts and Flowers, will speak
             on romance in the eighties.

DATE/TIME: Thursday, February 14 (Valentine's Day)
             12 noon

LOCATION: Browsers Bookstore
             312 Main Street
             Northampton

NOTES: There is no charge for this event and the public is invited.

             Mary Todd, a well-known authority on our changing society,
             currently teaches at Marion College in Indiana. She is the
             author of other books, including The Children of Today and
             and Love or Infatuation?

             Next Thursday's lunchtime program will be Hugh Smith, author
             of Auto Mechanics and You, talking about do-it-yourself car
             repair.

                                  -0-

<u>(TIP SHEET)</u>

Contact: Kathy Tyler
           First National Bank
           500 South Street
           Sioux Falls, South Dakota   57102

           (605) 555-6189

                              FOR IMMEDIATE RELEASE

          FREE WORKSHOP FOR WOMEN INTERESTED IN FINANCIAL CAREERS

               TO BE HELD AT THE FIRST NATIONAL BANK

EVENT: Free workshop for women interested in learning about careers
                 in banking and finance.

DATE/TIME: Thursday, April 3
                 5:30 p.m.

LOCATION: First National Bank Auditorium
                 500 South Street
                 Sioux Falls

ADDITIONAL
  INFORMATION: The workshop is free, but advanced registration is requested.
                 Call 555-6189 for reservations.

                 Where the jobs are, what to expect and what qualifications are
                 necessary for careers in banking and finance are just some of
                 the questions to be answered by guest speaker, Muriel Adams,
                 a career consultant.

                 For additional information, call Kathy Tyler at the First
                 National Bank, 555-6189.

                              -0-

THE BIOGRAPHY PRESS RELEASE

The biography press release is exactly that--a release telling the life story or the background of a particular person. Most companies have bios--as they are called--on all their senior management.

Do business owners and professionals need bios? In some cases, yes, a bio can be a good addition to your press material. It may stimulate press interest in your personal background giving you yet another opportunity to attract the attention of the media.

Who doesn't need a bio? Business owners who ARE their businesses usually don't need them. If the background of the business is almost totally intertwined with the background of the proprietor, then generally, enough information will have been provided in the background press release on the business. Joan Dorman Davis, the freelance college counselor (see pages 36-37.) is a good example of someone whose business is so personal that a separate bio would probably be of little use.

However, for the business owner who runs a shop or restaurant or who buys a franchise or takes over the family business, it makes excellent sense to have press material explaining who you are. Then your bio will answer, "Who is the person behind this business?"

Sample Biography Press Releases (See the following pages)

There are two forms of bios. The first is short and to the point, giving dates, schools attended and jobs held. The second type of bio is more detailed and is written in a feature story style.

(BIO: SHORT FORM)

Contact: Lynn Bower
           American Realtors/Bower Realty
           1011 Long River Drive
           Indianapolis, Indiana 46206

           (317) 555-0020

                    LYNN BOWER

    Lynn Bower is owner and operator of Bower Realty which is a member of
the nationwide American Realtors franchise system. Ms. Bower has run her
own real estate firm since 1975. She picked up the American Realtors franchise
to add to her operation in 1977.

    Her first job in the real estate industry was as a secretary with Cooper
Realty. She earned her state license to sell in 1963 and sold real estate for
Cooper Realty for six years before moving to Finest Homes in 1969. She
worked there until '75 when she decided to branch out on her own.

    Ms. Bower is President of Working Women of Indianapolis and serves
on the board of the local arts center.

    A native of Springfield, Illinois, Lynn Bower is a graduate of
Indiana University. She settled in Indianapolis permanently following her
graduation.

    Lynn Bower is married and has two children.

                    -0-

Contact: Dorothy Glenn
          Moss, Finley and Tupper
          510 Court Street
          Cleveland, Ohio 44114
          (216) 555-3267

RON FINLEY

By day, Ron Finley sits in a wood-paneled office meeting with clients, discussing financial planning and poring over figures. By night, Finley dons make-up and costume and assumes any number of roles.

When meeting Ron Finley, a partner in the accounting firm of Moss, Finley and Tupper, one would hardly suspect he is the same Ron Finley who performs professionally in many productions at the Hayden Playhouse in Cleveland. At 6'2", Finley traditionally wears pin-stripe suits and sports a distinguished salt-and-pepper beard. He looks far more the businessman than the actor.

To Finley this split life is the most natural thing in the world. "I love my work at the office. I enjoy meeting with people and solving the complexities involved in managing money," he says. "But at night I become a very different person--taking on new roles is a challenge I enjoy immensely."

Finley's schedule is a challenge as well. Hayden Playhouse performances are held Friday and Saturday nights and Sunday afternoons. Each play usually runs four weeks. Prior to the run, Finley's evenings are filled with rehearsals. "Tax time is the only time when I can't work at the Playhouse. We're just too busy here," he explains. "Otherwise I love the schedule. I can't think of a better place than the theatre to spend the rest of my time."

Finley was bitten by the acting bug six years ago while helping the Playhouse with its initial fundraising drive. It was the classic cliché when director Alfred Bush asked, "Ron, have you ever considered acting?" Finley has been at it ever since. His most recent role was as the doctor in A Doll's House.

Ron Finley helped form Moss, Finley and Tupper twelve years ago. A 1946 graduate of Ohio University, he is single and resides on Northridge Drive.

-0-

COVER LETTERS--WHEN TO USE THEM AND WHAT TO SAY

A cover letter personally addressed to a member of the media can be extremely helpful in bringing your press material to the attention of a particular producer, editor or reporter. In most cases, the letter is a nice personal touch, but not absolutely necessary.

The specific times when a brief covering note or letter might increase your chances of press coverage are the following:

1. If you have spoken to a member of the media and they have expressed interest in your story, then a cover note reminding them of your discussion and that they requested press information from you would be very important. A handwritten note would be perfectly satisfactory: "Good to talk to you this morning. Enclosed is the material we discussed concerning the possible story about my all-female radio station."

2. At other times, a cover letter can tell a particular reporter or producer why your story is just right for their medium. In this case, a cover letter is actually a shortcut. Rather than going to the trouble to write a release directed at a specific program, for example, you can send out your regular background press release with a cover letter explaining exactly what you have to offer their program or publication.

Let's take some examples. Suppose you are a personal financial advisor who runs your own business, and you'd like to appear on television talking about how people can best cope with inflation. Your best bet then for enticing a producer will be a cover letter describing why you would be a good guest. The letter should be accompanied by supporting material such as your press release and brochure. Your letter should be brief and to the point:

Dear _____;

    With inflation raging at 13 percent right now, most people are having difficulty managing their money. Yet many have persisted in keeping their cash in regular savings accounts earning only 5½ percent interest. Even for the small investor there are many other types of investments which offer a better hedge against inflation.

    From the conservative who invests in money market funds (paying a fluctuating 10½ percent interest) to the adventurous such as the woman who makes less than $15,000 but still manages to invest one-quarter of her paycheck in art and hopes to double and triple her investment, investors are finding ways to maximize their money during these inflationary times. I think your viewers would be interested in learning more about how even a small amount of savings can be put to work in the fight against inflation.

    As a guest on _____, I would be able to offer advice on some of the more common investments as well as the riskier ventures. If it would be helpful, one or two of my clients have said they would be willing to appear with me to discuss how inflation has affected them.

    "How the small investor can survive inflation" would provide helpful information for viewers of _____. Enclosed you will find information on my background. I'll look forward to hearing from you.

                     Sincerely,

    Simpler cover letters are also very much in order. The following letter from a pet store owner to a columnist who writes about house pets would serve as a simple letter of introduction as to why the store owner might be of value to the columnist:

Dear _____;

As owner of Pet World, I come in contact with all types of house pets from dogs and cats to parakeets, snakes, turtles, canaries and hamsters. My undergraduate training is in animal husbandry, and I am knowledgeable about house pet diseases. I also understand some of the mistakes owners make when choosing and trying to train a pet.

If you should ever need information for your column, please feel free to call me. I enclose background information on myself and the shop.

Sincerely,

Or if the store owner wants a specific type of article written about him, he might try the following:

Dear _____;

Did you know that the most common error people make when choosing a dog is not having taken time to examine their own needs thoroughly? Few people spend as much time choosing their pet as they would spend planning a family weekend away. Usually the first pair of big brown eyes that captivates a potential owner closes the sale. The new puppy goes home with them, and often there are mixed results. The owners discover that the dog grows much larger than their apartment can handle, or they learn that the puppy is a real yapper or even that he's prone to nipping.

Yet most of these pitfalls could be avoided if people would take a few hours to research breeds the way they research different makes of cars. Certain dogs are heavy shedders; others are going to grow into very large animals; still others are so notorious as barkers that many members of a particular breed have their voice boxes removed early in life.

The educated family will always be the happiest pet owners. After a few hours research, they can select the dog who will fit right in with their lifestyle.

If you would like to devote a column to this subject, I would be happy to provide you with any information you need. I enclose background information on myself and on Pet World.

Sincerely,

Occasionally, it may be <u>appropriate to write a letter to a reporter who has just done a piece in which you wish you had been included</u>. Immediately after the article has appeared is not too soon to make the reporter aware of you--for all you know, he or she may need to write a similar piece again in several months. The following letter is an example of what might be appropriate after a restaurant critic has done a piece about restaurants with beautiful decor:

Dear _____;

I enjoyed reading your recent article about the gorgeously designed restaurants of Denver. If you would like to try another type of beautiful dining spot, please come to A Little Bit of Louisiana, Denver's New Orleans-style restaurant.

Our Creole and Cajun cuisine is authentic, and it's quite a treat here in the Rockies. Our tin ceilings and fly fans help create the atmosphere of southern Louisiana. I think you should have the opportunity to see--and to taste--for yourself.

Please contact me at your convenience. I'll be happy to arrange for you to have lunch or dinner as our guest. I'll look forward to hearing from you. In the meantime, I'm enclosing some information on A Little Bit of Louisiana.

Sincerely,

At times, cover letters are the perfect touch for obtaining the publicity your business deserves, but let me remind you, <u>cover letters are by no means always necessary</u>. If you are doing a large mailing to announce news that speaks for itself (such as announcement of a new product, a staff promotion, a special event or an anniversary), then mailing out your press release alone will be fine.

THE PRESS KIT

A press kit is nothing more than a neat way of packaging all the material which might be of interest to the press.

When might you use it? A press kit could be given to any member of the press who is coming to do a story on your business. The kits are also convenient for distributing information to press people attending a special event. Members of the press will appreciate having all the material neatly organized for them.

The contents of a press kit will vary according to the occasion for which the kit is being prepared. If you're trying to interest a reporter in a feature story about your business, then you would include material such as your background press release and your biographical information. However, if you're preparing press kits to be distributed at a special event, then the primary contents of the kit will be items pertaining to the event. (On such occasions, always supplement the material on the event with background information on you and your business.)

Depending on the occasion, your press kit might include some or all of the following:

- Press releases (your background release plus any special releases pertaining to the occasion)

- Tip sheet (for an event)

- Bio

- Photo (if pertinent)

- Copies of any previous publicity you have received

- Your company brochure

- Any other items which you feel would be of interest

To neatly package your information, buy folders (perhaps in colors which complement your business colors) at a stationery store. Folders with pockets are particularly handy since there is a place to insert your materials, but a plain file folder will also be satisfactory.

To complete the package, a label can be used on the exterior of the folder to identify the contents of the press kit, and one of your business cards should be stapled to the inner pocket or the inside of the folder itself.

Chapter VI

THE IMPORTANCE OF PHOTOGRAPHS

We've all heard that "a picture is worth a thousand words," and perhaps nowhere is that more true than when approaching an editor who is reading thousands and thousands of words every day. If your story lends itself to the visual and can be told with a good photograph, you will do well to invest time or money in getting a good picture taken.

"But I thought newspapers send their own photographers..." you may be saying. You're right. Many do. Major newspapers and magazines rely almost totally on their own photographers or freelance stringers who work regularly for them. However, to consider the impact of a photograph sent to these publications, put yourself in an editor's shoes. Which would you rather look at---a two-page press release or a photograph? Most of us would be attracted to the picture. Even if the publication eventually sends its own photographer, the original photo you sent demonstrates to them the visual possibilities of your business.

And to the small newspaper without a staff of photographers, your picture will seem like water in a desert wasteland. Small publications need photographs desperately. If it's a choice between printing a press release or printing a photo with a caption, the photo will almost certainly win out. Why? Because the editors know that the reader, too, would rather have a picture tell the story---a photograph will be among the first things on the page to grab the reader's attention.

WHO WILL TAKE THE PHOTOGRAPH?

Some of you may be fortunate enough to have the skills to do your own photography. However, most of us will need to find a friend or a freelance photographer who can come take the photo for us.

If you are fortunate enough to have a friend with a 35mm camera who would be willing to spend an afternoon taking some photos, that's terrific. If not, cities abound with photographers. To get the best price, you would be smart to contact a local college or art school where you might find talented individuals who will be more negotiable on price. You might also call the newspaper to see if any of the staff photographers freelance.

The Yellow Pages will also have listings under "photographers." Many of these will be studio photographers, so be sure to ask if they are equipped to do on-location publicity shots. If they can't help you, ask if they know of someone who can.

Though students and some freelancers will undoubtedly work for less, here are some rates which are typical for on-location photography in New York City. For these prices, you receive proofs(samples prints of the photos from which you select what you will pay to have printed):

$55.00 = 1½ hours (door to door) or one roll of shooting

$37.50 = each additional roll

$175.00 = half day of shooting

$250.00 = whole day of shooting

$3.00 = per print you want made from the proof sheet

These are Monday through Friday rates. There is an extra charge for overtime or for shooting outside the city. Incidentally, since some photographers do charge per roll, find out how many exposures are on the roll and then keep track--or ask to be notified--of when you may be starting a new one. You may not care $37.50-worth about having that last shot or two taken.

Once you've selected the photographer you'll be using, make him or her part of your team. You probably have a good idea of the type of photo you want, but consult with the photographer as well about what kind of shot will work best. After all, they are experts at what they do, and their eyes are well-trained to give you the best results possible.

WHAT MAKES A GOOD PICTURE?

In general, publicity photographs are best when there is interesting action taking place in the picture and when the number of people involved is limited.

As you have probably already observed, there is nothing more boring than a photo of five or six people facing the camera. The picture says nothing, and most readers probably won't even take time to glance at the caption (the written explanation of what is occurring in the photograph). The reason why this type

of photo doesn't work well is because it violates the general guidelines cited above. There is no action taking place to describe
the story visually, and there are too many people involved.

In contrast, one yoga teacher reports that she gets fantastic
mileage out of photographs of herself in various yoga positions.
To the uninitiated, these positions look like impossible body con-
tortions, and a photo like this can't help but attract attention.
As a result, the teacher gets good coverage in neighborhood newspapers where they will run the photograph complete with caption
telling the date and time of upcoming classes.

What kind of photo will best sum up your business? It all
depends. If your work involves working with clients in their
homes or offices, a good photo might be of you with another person
in the appropriate surroundings actually conducting business.
Or if your work involves charts and graphs, then perhaps the
picture should depict you alone going over that material.

If you run a children's toy or bookstore, then children
truly enjoying your store's surroundings might make a good
picture. In this case, since the children would be viewed as one
group it is perfectly all right to use several of them.

Also, it is not necessary that you be in the picture unless
it helps explain what is happening.

Many business owners are hesitant to involve their real
clients or customers in preparation of their publicity material,
and that is perfectly understandable. There is no reason why
you can't set up a situation with a friend and be photographed
with him or her rather than with a client. The important element

is <u>truth in representation</u>. If you send out a photo showing
you involved in some sort of work with a friend, <u>try to re-create</u>
<u>exactly what you would be doing if you were working with a real</u>
<u>client.</u> Use people with whom you feel comfortable, but make
sure the action depicted is accurate.

PHOTOS FOR PRODUCT PUBLICITY

As discussed earlier, a photograph can be very helpful
in publicizing a particular product. Rather than relying on
a written description, you can sell your product to an editor
by <u>showing</u> him what it is like.

The primary requirements for this type of photo are an
<u>uncluttered background</u> and <u>proper lighting.</u> The ease with
which this is accomplished will largely depend on the item
involved. A very small object or one that reflects the light
may require the expertise of a professional. Otherwise, if you
or a friend have been doing the photography, try shooting a roll
of film using more than one background or lighting arrangement.
You'll probably come out with a photo you can use.

PHOTO COVERAGE OF AN EVENT

An awards ceremony, a street festival, a contest, the
appearance of a local celebrity or any other type of special
event all <u>provide photo opportunities for the press.</u> If you
have a story which will be particularly interesting visually,
you may want to call the photo editor of your local newspaper to

see if he or she would like to receive information on it. If so, send either a press release or a tip sheet on the event.

If a photographer should be sent to cover the occasion, you have several responsibilities. First and foremost, you should be helpful in setting up whatever type of photograph interests the photographer. Remember, you're asking for free exposure, so it's important to accommodate the wishes of the publication's photographer.

You'll also need to provide the photographer with caption information. This means making a list of the people appearing in the photograph and providing the correct spelling of their names and their proper titles. It is preferable to list the people in the order in which they appear from left to right. If for some reason the photo arrangement changes at the last minute, be sure to discuss with the photographer the order in which people were standing. It can be as simple as noting after the appropriate name which man had a beard or which was wearing the plaid jacket. Just confirm with the photographer that you are in agreement on the characteristics being used for identification.

And of course, be considerate of the publication's photographer. If your event involves food or a meal of some type, offer the photographer a few minutes to enjoy the occasion. Members of the press work hard, and if your event is scheduled during lunchtime, this may be the only opportunity they'll have to eat. It's up to you to make sure the photographer leaves with a good feeling about the event.

If you are going to the expense of holding a special event, you might also consider hiring a freelance photographer to take photos for your own use. You may want to have them to put in a brochure or special sales literature or to use in a display.

Additional photographs may also be helpful in getting publicity. Trade publications and smaller newspapers usually don't have staff photographers, so they welcome the photographs that are sent them. If photographs of your event have been taken by a freelance photographer, then you'll be equipped with pictures for these publications. The end result will likely be additional publicity for your event.

THE PORTRAIT SHOT

A portrait shot (a photo of a person from the shoulders up) of you or of staff members can be useful for announcing promotions, awards or various community activities. And occasionally, a portrait shot can be helpful when trying to become a guest on a television program--the person booking the interviews may be favorably impressed if you look alert and energetic in a photo.

However, portrait photographs are by no means a required item. Your publicity campaign will do just fine without them.

If it's convenient and relatively inexpensive for you to have a photo of you and/or your key personnel taken, then there are certainly ways to use the pictures. But if you're trying to cut costs right now, then this could be done at a later date.

When ordering prints of a portrait shot, either a 5 x 7 or 4 x 5 glossy will be satisfactory for use by newspapers and magazines. An advantage to the 4 x 5 size is that it fits in a regular business envelope which will save on postage.

PERMISSION TO USE A PHOTOGRAPH

Professional public relations people are very conscious of getting proper permission from those who are involved in a photograph, and there's some reason for it. Employees do leave under not-so-favorable circumstances, and friendships disintegrate occasionally. If you have gotten proper permission, then you will have protected yourself against any possibility of negative repercussions.

The rule-of-thumb on this is that <u>if the action depicted is a news event</u> (an awards ceremony, a pie-eating contest, a street festival, etc.) then <u>no permission is required</u>. However if you're <u>staging a photograph to be used for promotional purposes, getting permission is advisable</u>. A simple permission form which could be used is the following:

I give (<u>the company name</u>) permission to use my picture for promotional purposes, <u>with or</u> without the use of my name. (If you object to use of your name, strike out the words "with or" above.)

SIGN HERE: Date:

  Address:

IF ABOVE INDIVIDUAL IS A MINOR, CONSENT OF PARENT OR LEGAL GUARDIAN:

As parent or legal guardian of _____, I consent to the above terms.

SIGN HERE: Date:

  Address:

ORDERING PRINTS

Photographs to be sent for use by publications should be 8 x 10 or 5 x 7 glossies. The portrait shot is the exception to this, and a 4 x 5 print is acceptable. Glossy rather than matte finish is preferable, because it provides a sharper photograph from which to print.

Prints developed by hand by your photographer are likely to be of excellent quality but rather expensive. With some sacrifice in clarity but considerable savings in cost, you can ask your photographer to provide you with a "copy negative." Then for about 20-25¢ a print (vs. the $1 or more for original prints), you can have machine prints made. To find a company who makes machine prints, try the Yellow Pages under "photo finishing," consult a local camera shop or ask your photographer.

THE CAPTION

The purpose of the caption is to describe the picture to the reader. It should succinctly state who, what, when, where and why. Be sure to provide correct information as to the names and titles of any people involved, as well as checking carefully to make sure the order they are in is described correctly.

The caption should be typed on a separate sheet of 8½ x 11 paper which will be glued or taped to the back of the photograph. The reason for preparing the caption separately is because in the production process at a publication, the photo may be sent to one area to be prepared for print while the caption needs to be sent to another. Never write on the back of a print. Pencils or ball point pens can push through the paper and ruin the photograph, and a felt tip pen can smear onto--and ruin--other prints.

The correct format for a caption is as follows:

Contact:

                              FOR IMMEDIATE RELEASE

SUMMARY HEADLINE

Dateline--The caption explains the action of the photo. Write in the
present tense to make it current. ("Andrew Smith presents Suzanne
Stephens with an award.") Identify people in the photo by listing them
from left to right.

                              -O-

Once the caption is written, it needs to be securely attached
to the photograph. The caption should be typed on either half of
an 8½ x 11 sheet of paper (the stationery you are using for your
press releases would be just right for this). Then glue the
blank half to the back of the photograph so that both the photo
and caption are face up. Once you have attached the paper to
the photo, simply fold the other half of the letterhead over the
photograph, and the caption and photo will easily fit into a
manila envelope for mailing. Be sure to insert some stiff backing
like cardboard into each envelope you send to prevent damage
in the mail.

The Media

THE MEDIA

For some of us, there's something about "the media" which
may seem a bit intimidating. Perhaps it's the image of the press
which we get from movies and television. After seeing All The
President's Men or watching Lou Grant, one would hardly think
that Robert Redford, Dustin Hoffman or Ed Asner are sitting
around the City Room dying to hear from entrepreneurs who would
like to pitch stories about their businesses.

Fortunately for us, fictionalized depictions of the working
press romanticize reality. The truth of the matter is that
members of the media--from your local reporter to the national
magazine editor--are hungry to get their teeth into a new and
different story about an interesting person or event. What's
more, they are normal people like you or your neighbor, and
they are interested in much the same sort of story which would
be of interest to you.

"We're constantly looking for good stories," says an editor
at Us magazine. "At story meetings we're always trying to determine what's going on all over the country. Staff members are

assigned to read a certain number of local newspapers because we really need those different ideas."

The editor, who at one time worked as a reporter for a local newspaper, notes that the situation is no different there: "I was always looking for new story angles. If people sent me a concise presentation about something or someone unusual, I always tried to cover it if I could."

The press needs you as much as you need them. After all, if there weren't people like you out there starting new businesses or putting together worthwhile organizations, what would the press report on? If you approach the media properly with a well-thought out idea, your story will be difficult to resist.

This section will examine in depth how to approach the press. Along with general guidelines about the media, this section includes specific suggestions as to how to contact the various types of publications and programs. Also included are suggestions on how to prepare for a media interview.

Chapter VII

WORKING WITH THE PRESS

First of all, you need a basic understanding of the steps you will take time and again when you want to contact the media.

THE CONTACT PROCESS

For each press release you send out, you will:

☐ 1. Decide on the message. What is your press release going to say?

☐ 2. Select the media to be approached. (This could be one publication or program for a specific story, or it could be 25-50 different media for a general release.)

☐ 3. Prepare or select proper written material. (See "The Basics.")

☐ 4. Find out to whom the material should be sent. (If you don't know, call and ask.)

☐ 5. Determine proper timing if necessary.

☐ 6. Send material.

☐ 7. Follow up with a phone call if appropriate.

☐ 8. Send a thank you note for publicity received.

In the course of reading this chapter you will come to understand each of these steps more fully. And later, when your publicity program is well underway, this is the step-by-step process to which you will always return.

In order to effectively pursue the contact process, you now need more information about the working press themselves. Let's continue with our discussion.

RESPECT THEIR SITUATION

Press people--whether they work for a magazine, a newspaper or a radio or TV station--are exceptionally busy people. They usually have more work to do than is comfortable, and more often that not, they are working against a deadline. They are open to hearing from you, but it's important that you are respectful of the conditions under which they work.

Following these guidelines should help you make a favorable impression:

Respect their time. They will be grateful to you for doing so.

Understand their needs. As stressed in "The Basics," you need to spell out why your story is right for a particular medium. Some business owners succeed with doing blanket mailings to all the press in the area, but in general, you're going to fare better if your press release or the attached cover letter makes it clear why you are of interest to readers, viewers or listeners of that particular medium. If you've taken the time to understand the types of stories they cover, your suggestion will have a good chance of being picked up.

Understanding their needs also gives you flexibility. If publicizing a boutique, you don't have to restrain your publicity efforts to the fashion pages. Once you understand the publication, you may find an angle which will attract the attention of a "lifestyles" writer or even the architecture critic.

Follow the publication and avoid duplication of material. If a gardening columnist has just done an article about how African violets can be a frustrating plant to raise, you should be in tune with his feelings. Rather than mailing out a press release on violets which you've just written to promote your garden shop, you might write a letter or a new release suggesting a similar plant which is easier to care for. The columnist will be impressed that you have read and reacted to his column. (Even long-time journalists enjoy knowing that they have an impact on readers!) He may or may not do a column about the plant you suggested, but he'll likely keep you in mind as a source for other information. Why? Because you've flattered him by showing that you're an interested reader.

Re-evaluate your press material. Is it worthy of their attention? (Don't send press information on a marginal subject to a potentially valuable contact.) Is your material neatly typed? Concise? Easy to read? Does it explain why your story is right for their medium?

Take them at their word. If a reporter or producer asks you to call them at a certain time, they mean it. Call at the appointed hour. Or if they ask you to send them more information, do so that day. They don't have time to play games, and they never say anything "to be nice." One editor at McCall's tells a sad story of a woman who failed to follow up with what was requested. She had submitted press information on a new type of sewing machine, and when the magazine asked her to send samples of the work it could do, she never did---thus killing all chance of nationwide publicity.

If you are speaking to a member of the press on the phone or in person, don't press your cause too hard. No one likes to be pushed into a commitment or feel that they were tricked into some sort of an agreement. Present the positive aspects of your idea, and then let the material you've given them do your selling.

Don't send press information on the same subject to more than one person at each program or publication until you have a definite rejection from the person who received it first. On more than one occasion, I have seen the exact same story printed on the same day in different sections of a major daily newspaper. Because different editors oversee the various sections of the paper, no one noticed that the same press release had been sent to two separate departments. Though the newspaper should have caught it, the publicist was silly to run the risk of this happening---he or she can be guaranteed that the situation made everyone unhappy.

If a member of the media invites you to come in for an interview or makes an appointment to come to do a story on you, be prepared to make their job as easy as possible. They may very well need a basic explanation of your industry, type of business or organization or a rundown on some aspect of the field. Try to explain these subjects clearly (without being condescending)---after all, the press can't be experts on everything!

Any written material with which you can provide them will be appreciated. If they ask for anything more, send it to them as soon as you can. And be respectful of their wishes. If they want a tour of premises (or don't have time for one), accommodate them.

If you do receive a story in print or an interview on radio or televison, a thank you note is very much in order. It will help them remember you and want to work with you again.

WHO SHOULD RECEIVE YOUR MATERIAL?

If you've become familiar with the newspapers, magazines and radio and television programs which will be important to you, then you should already have some idea as to who should receive your press information. If a particular column or section of a magazine or newspaper carries a <u>byline</u>, then material should be sent to that person. Or if one print, radio or TV reporter specializes in your type of story, then that's the person to approach.

For other situations where you have no particular person in mind, it's still <u>important to direct the material to a specific person</u>. (Needless to say, the impact of mail which is personally addressed is far greater than an envelope sent to "Editor.") Here are some guidelines for determining who that person should be:

<u>Major newspapers</u> and <u>magazines</u> are usually divided into departments, and you'll want to direct your press information to the <u>editor of the proper department</u>. If you're not certain where your story would fit in, <u>call and ask</u>: "I'm sending some material regarding _____, and I would like to know to whom I should send it." It's to their advantage to help you, because it will save them time if the information is sent to the right person in the first place.

<u>Radio and television news programs</u> have <u>news directors</u> or <u>assignment editors</u> who are responsible for handing out assignments. <u>Call to find out the name of this person.</u>

Guests for radio and television <u>talk shows</u> may be selected by a <u>producer</u>, a <u>talent coordinator</u> or by the <u>host</u> or <u>hostess</u>. You'll need to learn the system for each program you approach.

Neighborhood newspapers and special interest publications are usually published by just a handful of people. The name of the editor here may produce a valuable contact for you.

If you are sending out publicity on a special event or other material which may become dated within a matter of days, be sure your contact isn't out with the flu or away on vacation. You may need to get another name, or--in this instance-- you could send material to "Events Editor" or Assignment Editor" in order to assure that your material is opened on receipt.

Also, keep in mind that in large cities where radio, TV and newspaper reporters have large areas to cover (like covering "the arts" in New York City), they sometimes have assistants who work closely with them. It can be to your advantage to direct your material to the behind-the-scenes person instead of the reporter. The assistant probably receives fewer personally addressed pieces of mail, so your release may receive special attention. And though he or she probably doesn't make the final decision, the assistant will certainly see that your material gets fair consideration.

HOW TO ATTRACT PRESS ATTENTION

Unfortunately, your press release is just one among many others vying for attention. One producer of a radio program in New York says that on Monday morning her stack of mail can be a foot high. You do have competition, but if you're offering something fresh and different, you'll still stand a good chance of getting your story. The biggest danger you face is that your material might be misdirected or inadvertently mis-placed before the right person has even had the opportunity to consider it.

Here are some suggestions for helping it <u>get to the right place and attract favorable attention as well</u>.

The <u>look of the envelope</u> can help to make your letter among the first that are opened. If it is <u>neatly typed</u> and <u>personally addressed</u>, it adds interest for the person opening the mail. (You'd be surprised at the amount of mail press people receive from computer print-outs or directed to "Editor." They feel about it much the way you probably feel about the "junk mail" you receive.)

If you have a particularly important idea you're trying to publicize, you might also consider <u>having the material hand-delivered</u>. Some members of the press say this adds importance to the item. It should also assure you that the material was, indeed, received by the right person.

If you live in a large city, you can use <u>messenger services</u>; or regardless of where you live, you could use a <u>high school student</u> or consider <u>delivering it yourself</u>. This special attention is usually not necessary for most press information, but if you have a particular publication where you'd really like exposure, you might consider this as another way to draw attention to the importance of your material.

<u>PHONING THE PRESS</u>

The telephone is your handiest--and quickest--link to the media. Here are some things you should know.

If you simply want to <u>call to find out to whom to send the material</u>, ask for the publisher's office (magazine) or the <u>producer's office</u> (radio or television talk show) or the <u>news</u>

<u>desk</u> (newspaper and radio or television news shows). The people
who answer the phones in these locations should be able to tell
you what you need to know. <u>Early in the day is generally best</u>
for this type of call. But needless to say, if you're phoning a
morning talk show which is broadcast from 9-10 a.m., don't phone
first thing in the morning. A program like that would be better
prepared to handle calls from about 11 a.m. on.

At times, you may want to phone a reporter, editor or
producer directly <u>to see if they are interested in a certain</u>
<u>subject before sending out your material</u>. This would be entirely
appropriate if your material will date quickly. That way if
one reporter isn't interested in the subject, you can go on
to contact someone else.

The most considerate way to make this type of phone call
is like this: "I'm _____, and I would like to discuss _____
with you. Do you have a minute to talk about it now?" If
they have a few minutes, they'll talk to you then, but if they
are working on deadline, you've given them the opportunity
to ask you to call back.

Publicists are always taught that it's important to <u>follow</u>
<u>up with a phone call after sending out press material</u>, and they
learn to ask: "Have you seen the material I sent you about _____?"
This should elicit comments from the reporter or editor without
backing him into making a commitment. Always avoid asking:
"Are you coming?" or "Will you do the story?" No one likes to
be pinned down, and if they say "no" you have little recourse.
By simply having a general conversation, you should be able to

keep the door open and perhaps eventually get a "yes" or a "maybe."

I have mixed emotions about follow-up phone calls. I <u>do</u> think they help, but I also know that most of you are short on time. As a rule of thumb I would suggest this: If an article in a particular publication or an interview on a special program will <u>make a big difference to your business or organization,</u> then <u>you should make a follow-up phone call a definite priority</u> for you or a staff member. However, if you're doing a large, general press mailing on a new product announcement or a staff promotion, then I think you can safely forget about phoning.

If you do call, what you're hoping to accomplish is to <u>rekindle their interest</u> in the material and <u>give them the oppor-tunity to ask for more information</u> in order to do the story. And if for some reason they weren't intrigued with the material, it provides you with the chance to get <u>first-hand feedback as to what would work better</u> for their program or publication.

When you do phone:

-<u>Know exactly what you want to say</u>. Make notes if necessary. (Many reporters and editor answer their own phones, so don't be surprised if you get through to them immediately.)

-<u>Think through answers to any questions</u> you think they might ask.

-If they request information, <u>send it immediately</u>.

<u>HOW TO TIME YOUR PRESS MATERIAL</u>

For many types of publicity, <u>the timing is unimportant</u>. You can mail the releases at any time, and the material can be used at the convenience of the program or publication.

However, when publicizing a special event or mailing out "timely" releases (see "The Basics"), it will be vital to pay attention to the timing.

Here, the best advice I can give you is to identify the media to whom you'll be directing the releases, and then call to get some idea of their publication or program schedules. (Refer to page 125 for suggestions regarding an organized method for keeping track of this information.) A monthly magazine can close as much as 3-4 months before the date it comes out, while a daily newspaper can insert material up until the night before the paper appears.

In general, you'll probably find that a daily newspaper and the radio and television news programs want material approximately one week in advance, while weekly publications will need to receive material 2-3 weeks beforehand. But rather than relying on these general guidelines, call your local media to be sure. It would be a shame to miss getting exposure simply because the material arrived too late.

HOW TO DEVELOP A PRESS LIST

Once your publicity program is underway, you'll probably find that you'll be working with the same reporters and media again and again. When you've assembled names and addresses for your first press mailing, you'll have created your basic press list.

I find that keeping my entire press list on 3 x 5 index

cards works well. Each reporter and/or publication or program gets a separate card that reads something like this:

```
Name:
Publication or Program:
Address:

Phone:
Notes:   Here I keep track of such things as:
         -how far in advance to submit timely material
         -whether they've done a story based on my material or
          whether they've attended an event I worked on
         -specific likes and dislikes
```

You'll find this system can be very handy. If you're sending out a big press mailing, you can simply sort through the cards and select the people who should receive the material. Then a secretary or temp worker can prepare envelopes from the cards you indicate.

The card system also makes it easy to keep an up-to-date list. If a reporter is no longer with a certain publication, you can cross out the name or make up an entirely new card without ever having to re-do an entire list.

Chapter VIII

SPECIFICS ABOUT THE VARIOUS MEDIA OUTLETS

The material covered thus far in "The Media" gives you
all the basic information you need for getting in touch with
the press. Now here are some additional suggestions, tips
and reminders about the various types of media. As you'll see
from this list, there's no shortage of outlets for your
press information!

NEWSPAPERS

Your town's <u>local daily newspapers</u>, the <u>major newspapers
in a nearby city</u>, <u>regional papers</u> and any <u>weekly neighborhood or community papers</u> in your area are the ones you'll
want to include in your press list. <u>Check newsstands or
the library</u> to be sure you know of all the papers distributed
in your area.

Remember, major newspapers are organized by departments,
and each department is responsible for assembling certain
sections of the paper. Your first step with each release
you wish to send out is to <u>determine the appropriate section</u>
where it belongs (for example, "sports," "style," "metropolitan
news," "the arts," etc.) Look for a regular <u>byline</u> in that
section, or call and ask for the name of the <u>editor</u> in that

department. If after looking at the paper, you're unsure
as to which section should receive your material, call and
describe the nature of your release and ask to whom such
information should be directed.

Neighborhood or community newspapers are usually put
out weekly by very small staffs. Their quietest day--and
the best day for phoning them--is the day their paper is
distributed. <u>Photographs generally increase your chance
of coverage</u> here. And <u>a story of particular significance
to community residents</u> will also have a better chance of
being picked up.

Addresses for all newspapers can be found on the individual
mastheads or in the local telephone book.

MAGAZINES

Like newspapers, magazines are also organized by department.
At major publications, different editors oversee various
departments, while at smaller publications, one editor or
managing editor will generally oversee everything.

After studying a magazine, you may find a <u>bylined writer</u>
who seems like the right person to receive your particular
release. If so, staff writers can be contacted by writing or
phoning the publication. If you suspect that a particular
writer whom you'd like to contact is a freelancer, you can
sometimes contact him or her by sending a letter care of
the publication, or call to get a phone number and address.

If no writer seems right for receiving your material,
<u>call the publication to get the name of an editor to whom
your information could be sent</u>.

Magazine <u>deadlines need to be watched closely</u> when mailing
timely material. Depending on their production schedule,

magazines close anywhere from two weeks to four months ahead
of time. Call to learn the schedule of the magazines on your
press list.

Before submitting material, be sure to check newsstands or
the library to become familiar with the magazines where you're
sending your release.

Among the types of magazines which you may be considering
as possible outlets for publicity are:

- City magazines (publications designed to provide information
  for residents of a particular city): These magazines are
  usually eager for material of local interest and are
  excellent publicity outlets.

- National news magazines (Time, Newsweek, etc.): These publications need hard-hitting news from their sources. If you
  have startling facts of national significance, you may
  be able to break in.

- National general and special interest magazines (Us, People,
  the women's magazines such as Glamour, Vogue, and Working
  Woman as well as Gourmet, Psychology Today, Esquire,
  Sports Illustrated, etc.): If your business relates to
  the type of information covered in one of these publications,
  then you may have a good shot at getting publicity. Think
  through your news angle carefully and be sure it's of
  national interest. Then take time to determine which
  department should receive your material. These publications
  use a great deal of material and are always eager to hear
  from business owners and professionals throughout the
  country.

TRADE PUBLICATIONS

You're no doubt familiar with the industry publications for
your field, but there may be other trade publications where it
would be appropriate to send your publicity. For those publications

in other fields, ask friends and associates for suggestions or
check one of the media directories recommended in the "Resources"
section, page 169.

These publications are almost always glad to receive news
which would be of interest to their readers. Because they are
staffed by only a few people, your release will sometimes
appear word-for-word as you have written it. The person on
the masthead listed as "editor" or "managing editor" is
generally the right person to approach.

Take time to understand the type of news they cover like
staff promotions or new business developments. (To get sample
copies to study, ask friends, check the library or write directly
to the publication and request a sample copy.) Then keep
them up-to-date on the happenings within your organization.

ASSOCIATION PUBLICATIONS

Your alumni association publication or the magazines or
newsletters sent out by any clubs or professional organizations
of which you are a member are ideal places for sending news of
you and your business. Again, research the kind of material
each publication tends to print, and then send appropriate
press releases to the editor or managing editor.

COMMUNITY PRESS

If you have news of local interest, then there are still
more outlets for your publicity. The local college newspaper,
the newsletters of the YM- or YWCA, the Chamber of Commerce
magazine or any community publications may be other good
places to send releases. Check with the organizations in your
community, and if they have a publication which seems right to
you, add them to your press list.

WIRE SERVICES

Wire services--the largest of which are the Associated
Press and United Press International--distribute news and

features of national interest to newspapers nationwide.
They operate in much the same fashion as newspapers. If you
have material which might be of interest to AP or UPI, check
the phone book to see if there is a bureau for each wire service
in your town, or check to see if they are located in the largest
city nearby. If not, ask your newspaper for the location of the
nearest AP and UPI bureaus. You can also inquire at the New
York offices. (For addresses, see the <u>Media Directory</u>.) <u>Each
regional bureau usually assigns the stories for that area of
the United States, so it's important that you contact the offices
nearest you</u>. Once you have found the locations of each wire
service's nearest bureau, phone to learn to whom your releases
should be sent.

SYNDICATED SERVICES

A syndicate operates in much the same way as a newspaper,
but like a wire service, <u>the material chosen for national distribution by syndication must be of more than local interest.</u>

Most syndicates are located in the major cities on the East
and West coasts, and they are sometimes <u>connected with one of
the major newspapers</u> (<u>The New York Times</u>, <u>The New York Daily
News</u>, <u>The Los Angeles Times</u>, etc.). Business owners who
receive publicity in a newspaper which operates a syndication
service sometimes learn later that their story appeared in
papers all over the country--and they didn't have to do a thing!

In addition to the services run by major papers, <u>there are
some special interest syndicates</u> whose addresses are listed
in the Media Resource Directory.

<u>The newspaper-run syndicates usually take material which has
already run in the parent paper</u>. People who get nationwide exposure through this type of syndicate usually haven't had to make
any special effort--the story simply caught the eye of the syndication editor once the story appeared in the parent paper.
However, if a reporter from such a paper is doing a story about you,
and you'd like national exposure, <u>ask the procedure</u> for being
considered for syndication. <u>For the special interest syndicates,
your approach is the same as for a newspaper or wire service.</u>

RADIO AND TELEVISION

You can get a <u>complete listing</u> of all the AM, FM and TV <u>stations in your area from the newspaper</u>. Then get phone numbers and addresses from the telephone book.

If there are particular programs or personalities to whom you want to send material, be sure to <u>set up a separate press list card for each one</u> as programs within one station will be planned by completely separate staffs.

Remember to <u>watch or listen to a particular program</u> before submitting material. <u>Determine why you would be a good guest</u> and what you would like to talk about. Then find out who is in charge of <u>scheduling guests for a talk show</u> (producer, host or talent coordinator) or in charge of <u>making assignments for a news program</u> (news director or assignment editor). <u>Send written material</u> explaining why you would be a good guest, and be prepared to stress your strengths in a <u>follow-up phone call</u>.

Sometimes, you can also increase your chances for becoming a guest on a talk show by offering to be available to <u>fill in at the last minute</u> or to be <u>booked during the slow times</u> (usually in August and around the holidays).

You may find that the person responsible for booking a program may phone you and want to chat. This is known as the "pre-interview" and you need to be as enthusiastic and well-informed during this discussion as you would be for the pro-gram---they're testing to see if you'll make a good guest.

Television is a <u>visual medium</u>, so be sure to mention any-thing you can <u>show</u> or <u>demonstrate</u> when contacting the tele-vision talk shows or news programs.

For either radio or television, the following would apply. If a news director or assignment editor for a news program likes your idea and says they will send someone out:
   -find out if they expect anything specific (like members
    of the band organized to play a special number or the
    dance troupe in costume for a period dance, etc.) By
    learning the angle they intend to take, you'll be better
    prepared for their arrival.

If a producer or host invites you to come to the studio
to be a guest on a talk show, be sure to ask:
    -How long is your segment of the show?
    -Exactly what subject is to be discussed?
    -Will you be part of a panel?
    -Is it taped or live?
    -Whom should you contact upon arrival?

National radio and television talk shows are put together
in exactly the same manner as a local program. A talent
coordinator or associate producer usually handles the booking
of guests rather than the producer or host, but for you the
contact process will be the same. Of course, your news should
be of national interest if you are approaching Good Morning,
America, The Today Show or Phil Donahue, for example.

THE COLUMNIST, THE CRITIC AND THE FREELANCE WRITER

The columnist, the critic and the freelance writer are
all members of the media who function in special ways, and
they may prove to be important to you. Whether affiliated
with a magazine, newspaper, syndication service or even
radio or television, each of these types functions in a
predictable way. We'll touch upon each of them separately.

The Columnist

Columnists range from the nationally syndicated "Dear Abby"
to the regional gardening columnist or the writer who assembles
your newspaper's "new and useful" product columns.

Columnists usually want complete exclusivity on a story, so
if you think your news is just right for a particular columnist,
you'll want to send your material to that writer only. Note
that it is being offered to them on an exclusive basis. Then
you'll need to get a definite "yes" or "no" before approaching
anyone else. To encourage a reply, enclose a self-addressed
stamped postcard with boxes to be checked off depending upon
the reaction. You may also need to follow up by phone. Or

consider offering the material exclusively "if used by December 3,"
for example. That way if you've been unable to contact the
columnist, you're still free to offer it elsewhere exclusively or
to send it out for general release. If one of the columnists to
whom you offer it wishes to use the material, wait until the
column has appeared. You are then free to send out the story for
general release.

Local columnists should be easy for you to contact at the
publication where they work. National magazine columnists can
also be approached through the publication where the column appears.

National newspaper columnists are generally distributed by
syndication. Some can be contacted by writing to them care of
the local publication where their column appears, but call your
local paper first to confirm that the letter will be forwarded.
Or you might ask someone at the newspaper for the address of the
syndicated service, so you can write directly.

The Critic or Reviewer

If you are trying to publicize a restaurant, theatre group or
some other type of business or organization where being reviewed
is important, then you'll want to know about approaching critics
and reviewers.

Some restaurant critics have a set system for the order in which
they review new dining spots. A television station in New York
simply accepts the material in the order in which it is received
and informs owners or publicists that it may be up to a year's
time before the critic gets around to visiting their establishment.
Your local publications may have a similar system, so call to
inquire. If so, you'll want to send them the necessary material
as quickly as possible.

Other times critics prefer to arrive unannounced, so they may
be vague as to how they select restaurants for review and when
they might choose to do so. Many restaurant owners keep photographs of local reviewers posted in the kitchen so that the
personnel will have the opportunity to recognize a critic who
arrives unannounced.

A theatre group or concert hall staff has a slightly different problem. They need to have a critic come to see a performance within a specific amount of time. Here, the best thing to do is to provide local critics with press information and complimentary tickets well in advance of the performances. Then follow up with a phone call to test the response and to see if more information is needed.

Regardless of whether a restaurant critic has responded to your invitation or whether a reviewer has attended a particular performance, be sure to keep them on your regular mailing list. The more familiar he or she becomes with your organization, the better off you'll be. You're building your image and strengthening your identity by keeping the critic informed.

Also, don't feel as if the only critic who counts is the one who works for the major daily newspaper in your area-- critics for neighborhood newspapers and special interest magazines can be equally valuable, and in general, it will be easier to catch their interest. Because local residents do turn to special publications like their neighborhood newspapers for information on local shopping specials and happenings of interest, a good review of a restaurant or a play may well spur them to action. It's still valuable publicity.

Should you always provide a complimentary meal or tickets for a critic? Yes, if you've invited them to come. However, if a critic prefers to arrive unannounced, then his or her employer is doubtless prepared to pick up the tab. It's still probably a good idea to offer a complimentary arrangement, and if that is refused, a restaurateur may still want to provide a free bottle of wine while a theatre publicist or owner might want to offer complimentary tickets to another play or performance.

In addition, remember that there are many ways other than reviews for getting publicity. Look for other angles about your business or organization. (See "The Basics.") If a restaurant has entertainment of some kind, that should be publicized. A dinner theatre should be actively promoting the people in the show as well as the play. For a concert hall, the architectural design which creates such fine acoustics might make a good story. Think about the other interesting aspects of your business or organization, then write up a press release or draft a cover letter and begin your approach to other members of the media. <u>This type of exposure can be equally important.</u>

The Freelance Writer

Besides notifying press staff members of your activities, another important person to stay in touch with is a freelance writer--perhaps you know one or have already been contacted by one. <u>They are always looking for fresh story ideas, too.</u>

There are advantages and disadvantages to working with freelancers. The main advantage is the possibility of greater exposure. A writer may interview a psychologist on job burnout and <u>spin that material off into articles for two or three of</u> his or her regular markets--anything from publicity in a trade publication to a national magazine may result!

The disadvantage concerns the fact that the writer <u>cannot guarantee placement</u> of a story. Even if he or she is working on a firm assignment, stories are often killed for reasons that have nothing to do with the quality of work. (Staff-written material is also killed at times, but probably less frequently.) You'll also find that freelancers will usually try to include you in an article in which he or she is doing several inter-views. Non-staffers tend to have difficulty selling profile pieces or articles examining only one business or organization.

Also, remember that freelancers expect no payment from you--they earn their money from the publication. By the same token, even if the writer is a good friend of yours, you can't expect the story to reflect any special favors. The writer has been hired to be objective and must try to remain so.

If you have the name of a local freelancer, he or she can probably be tracked down in your phone book. Otherwise, try

contacting the publication where you have seen their work. The
publication might forward your letter to them, or perhaps they'll
provide you with the writer's address and phone number.

Chapter IX

THE INTERVIEW AND AFTER

As your work pays off, interviews with the press will
become standard procedure for you--you won't think twice about
a quick chat with a reporter. But while getting started,
here are some tips to keep in mind.

HOW TO HANDLE AN INTERVIEW

- <u>Be prepared</u>. Think through the subject matter you expect
  to discuss, and come up with two or three good points to
  stress. (Specific points made during the interview are
  generally more helpful to the press than having a
  rambling discussion with them.)

- <u>Keep in mind the audience</u> of that particular medium.
  If certain information would be of special interest to
  that group, be sure to bring it up.

- <u>Be direct and friendly</u>.

- If you don't understand a question, <u>ask for clarification.</u>
  Don't just ramble on. Also, remember that it's perfectly
  all right to pause for a moment to formulate the proper
  answer.

- <u>Don't try to avoid answering questions</u>. The interviewer
  will sense that your're hiding something. (If you're

sensitive about any subject, think through the questions
they might ask you, and develop direct, honest answers
with which you're comfortable. That way nothing will
catch you by surprise.)

- Don't "sell." If the press has come to do a story about
  you, your product or service or a specific cause, give the
  reporter the time and space to become respectful of the
  situation himself. The media will always react negatively
  to a direct commercial "plug" from you.

- Relax and be yourself. If you're at ease, it will put the
  reporter at ease, and the result will be a better story.

For Radio and Television

- Sometimes publicists provide the host or producer of
  a radio or TV program with a list of suggested questions
  or some logical points to be discussed. If they are
  short on staff, this can be a real aid to them, and it
  helps you anticipate what to expect. (Of course, they
  may not use them, so be fully prepared anyway!)

- If you're appearing with other guests, avoid disagreements.
  Even if you're right, it's hard to look good when there
  is hostility.

- Speak slowly and distinctly.

- Any sort of nervous habit may jeopardize the interview,
  so be conscious of what you are likely to do and avoid it.
  On radio, finger-tapping can be picked up on the microphone,
  and swiveling back and forth in a chair sometimes makes it
  sound as if your voice is fading in and out. On television,
  these and other nervous habits can be very distracting to
  the viewer.

- Ask a friend to rehearse with you. Let him or her ask
  the questions you anticipate, and then practice answering
  concisely.

For Radio:
- Relax and feel comfortable. After all, it's generally
  only you and the interviewer in the studio.

For Television:
- TV cameras are getting better and better, but to be on
  the safe side wear plain-colored clothing (not white).
  Plaids, checks and small prints often don't pick up well
  on camera. Also avoid dangling jewelry or pieces which
  reflect the light---these can be distracting to the
  audience.

- Remember that television is a visual medium. If you have
  something to show or to demonstrate, it will make you a
  more interesting guest.

- Forget about the camera, and simply tell your story to
  the interviewer--as if you were chatting with a friend.

Above all, have a positive attitude: The interview will
work out well. Then you can relax and have a good time, and
after only an interview or two you'll begin to feel like an
old pro!

INTERVIEW RESULTS

Is there a way to predict---or to guarantee---the outcome
of an interview with the press? There isn't, I'm sorry to say.

From the moment you begin sending out press releases, it's
important that you understand that the media make the final

decisions about how the material is used and what is to
be said. In an ad, you pay for the space so you can control
everything from the message to the day and the time it is run.
With free publicity, those decisions are left in the hands of
the press.

But as we discussed in "Starting Up," it is this very
objectivity which makes publicity so valuable: An unbiased
observer has found your organization or business worthy
of his audience's attention.

If you've thought out your publicity campaign and
are well-prepared for the press, the articles which result
will reflect the time, thought and attention you've put into
your program.

HOW TO FIND OUT IF YOUR PUBLICITY BECOMES A STORY

In most cases, the best way to trace whether or not your
publicity is used is to enlist the help of friends, neighbors
and co-workers, and do the best you can to follow the various
programs and publications yourself.

Can you call the press to ask if your publicity was used?
NO! They're doing you a favor to run your story, and to hassle
them in this way is inexcusable. Their attitude is, "If you
don't read the publication, why do you want publicity in it?"

Of course, if a reporter has come to interview you, you
might ask for a general idea of when the story might run, but
after that, you should take the responsibility of watching for
it yourself.

If you're doing a large press mailing to many publications, there is every likelihood that you will receive publicity you never know about. (Major companies employ clipping services whose job it is to read magazines and newspapers nationwide and forward publicity to the client. However, these services tend to be expensive---there is both a per month and a per clipping charge.) If you're going to be sending press releases regularly to specific publications, it might be a good idea to take out subscriptions.

You will also find that asking clients and customers how they heard about you will provide a clue as to when and where you're achieving visibility.

BUILDING A RELATIONSHIP WITH A MEMBER OF THE MEDIA

Finally, a very important element in dealing with the media is building the contacts to facilitate future publicity efforts for you and your business.

Members of the media are people first and reporters second. If things click between you and a reporter, do what you can to further the relationship. You may want to invite them to lunch, take them to coffee or simply stay in touch on a regular basis.

Why is this so important? Though they may not be able to do another story for you for awhile, they may know of other reporters who are working on related pieces. They can also provide invaluable advice on getting in touch with other media.

And it's not just a one-way street. You may be able to

do favors for them, too. Perhaps they need suggestions on a
new story they're working on--you may know people to recommend
they talk to or have ideas as to where they can go for more
information on the subject. The favors you do will come full
circle back to you one day.

And while developing relationships, don't forget about
the assistant who may have helped you. Perhaps getting to
know him or her better is a good idea, too.

BEING PERSISTENT PAYS OFF

Persistence is the final ingredient for successful media
contact.

Sometimes a publication will like your idea immediately, and
first thing you know a word-for-word copy of your press release
will appear in the local paper. On other occasions, they won't
be interested, and you'll simply need to be persistent. Perhaps
you need to wait a month and send the reporter or editor a
slightly updated version of the same release; or you may need
to come up with a completely new angle for your next approach.
Intuition and common sense will be your best guides in each
situation.

Will persistence pay off? Absolutely! Everyone from
the publicist for a major corporation to the P.R. agency professional to other individuals like yourself have had their press
releases rejected or ignored by various publications at different
times. Maybe the editor was just having an off-day the first
time the press material arrived, or maybe the frequency of

seeing the material over and over again makes him feel more familiar with--and hence, more interested in--the subject.

One image consultant had been trying for months to break into one particular publication. She had been in touch on several occasions with the editor of the fashion section and several reporters who reported to that editor. Finally the editor assigned someone to do a two-page photo story on her. "What made you finally decide to do the story?" asked the image consultant.

"You were so persistent," was the editor's reply.

Those who stick with it and keep trying different story angles will find that there's a way to get into almost every media outlet you want to. Don't give up!

Your Image

YOUR IMAGE

There's an old P.R. agent story I'd like to share with you
because the message is something to keep in mind:

An out-of-breath P.R. agent rushes into a company meeting
where plans for a major event are obviously not going too well.
But the agent interrupts proudly, "Well, we've got stories in
The Post, The Times and The Daily News---"
"Now if only we could control the word of mouth," cuts in
one of the executives cynically.

In other words, no matter how well you do at getting publicity
for your business, the bottom line is that there needs to be
substance and a positive image behind it.

Some of the largest companies in the U.S. spend huge amounts
of money on publicity campaigns but never bother to train their
operators or secretaries to take phone messages politely. As
a customer, which is most important to you--reading about a
company in the newspaper or having your phone message taken
politely? And if you are treated rudely, what does this do to
your perception of the company?

Or consider for a moment the image of the Rolls Royce. The

mention of that name probably brings very similar pictures to both our minds: One usually thinks of a luxurious car driven by a person who enjoys the finer things in life and doesn't hesitate to spend money to get them.

All right, now suppose that the makers of the Rolls Royce decide to save money on car production by using a less expensive seat cover. However, the substitute seat covers split when exposed to the sun over long periods of time. Now wouldn't that ruin their image? It would destroy everything the company has done to build a reputation for excellence. No amount of savings could be worth risking that.

The same thing is true for the midtown doughnut shop whose press release stresses the company's efficiency and the product's freshness. The owner should do all that is necessary to assure that the baked goods are fresh and the service is always efficient. If a harried office worker waits too long to be served or finds that the doughnuts are stale, the shop may lose his patronage.

When identifying the strengths of your business for the purpose of preparing your press material, you probably came up with descriptions like "personal service," "thorough screening," "careful attention," "neighborhood atmosphere," "rarest delicacies" or "promptness." These are the sorts of things which contribute to the image you are building. Always take care to maintain them.

The restaurant owner who follows a consistent method of food preparation and provides an even level of excellence in service has little to worry about if a restaurant critic arrives unannounced.

This section is going to talk briefly about the other factors involved in building an image. Your personal visibility, the appearance of your store or office, the look of your stationery and sales literature as well as the attitude of your staff all contribute to how people perceive your company as a whole. No area should be neglected.

In addition, there may eventually come a time when you decide to explore having a public relations firm represent you. Hiring others to enhance your image and convey your message can be tricky business, and this section concludes with a chapter on "How and When To Hire an Outside Public Relations Firm."

Chapter X

HOW YOU AND YOUR COMPANY CAN BE

VIEWED POSITIVELY BY OTHERS

In all likelihood, you <u>are</u> your company. The activities
you choose to become involved in and the contacts you make can
directly affect your company's bottom line. This means that
giving thought to your personal image will be vital.

<u>YOUR PERSONAL IMAGE</u>

<u>Community activities and involvement demonstrate civic</u>
<u>spirit and increase your personal visibility</u>. By being active in
the Chamber of Commerce, the Rotary Club, trade associations or
church committees, you accomplish several things. First, you
<u>express to community members your concern for the city or town</u>
where you live. Others who are active in the community may make
a special effort to do business with you because of this. Another
benefit is that <u>members</u> of various organizations usually go to
some length <u>to do business with each other</u>, so you may pick
up customers in this way. And finally, there is usually some
form of <u>publicity</u> as a result of your participation. Aside
from your own <u>company press release</u> announcing your appointment
to a special committee or other such undertaking, <u>organization</u>
<u>newsletters</u>, <u>stationery letterhead</u> and <u>brochures often mention</u>
<u>the names and companies of active members</u>.

Public speaking is another way in which you can increase your visibility, further establish yourself as an expert in your field and possibly gain additional publicity.

Trade associations and professional organizations often need speakers on various topics. Direct mailings to members usually announce the speakers, and there are often newsletter-- and sometimes newspaper--reports on the event as well. By speaking in front of a variety of groups, you can broaden your sphere of influence.

Donate money, products or services to charitable organizations when possible. Such actions promote goodwill and usually increase your visibility. In some cases, you may want to publicize the donation yourself. Other times, as with charity auctions, the organization usually does a good job of spreading the word themselves.

Keep up your contacts. Many business owners feel, "I just don't have time to go to lunch with people..." Four days out of the week this may well be true, but I strongly recommend that you block out one day of the week when you meet people for lunch, dinner or drinks. You can meet friends, other professionals or seek out casual acquaintances whom you'd like to know better--- perhaps members of the press. Sometimes these meetings will result in nothing more than a pleasant break from your routine, but even then, the person whom you met with may get back to you several weeks later with a lead which will result in additional business. People tend to do business with people they know, so it's important to constantly be broadening your network.

HOW TO BE VIEWED AS AN EXPERT IN YOUR FIELD

How does a psychologist become known for her expertise on women and depression? How can a lawyer gain a reputation for estate planning? Many of the people I work with are professionals who ask questions such as these. In essence, we've talked about what needs to be done, but it may help to summarize.

Though it may seem odd, part of becoming known as an expert is becoming known as a good source. If a reporter is on deadline and calls you for a quick quote, be direct and to the point. If you're sensitive to their needs, they'll be calling back again.

More aggressive steps can be taken by sending out thoughtful press releases. (See "The Basics.") Trend and "timely" press releases (pages 75-86) are particularly good for suggesting subject matter which casts you as an authority. Those who are very comfortable with the written word might also consider donating a regular column or an article to local publications. However, this can require a great deal of work so unless you're a facile writer, tread cautiously here.

Also keep in mind what was just said about personal image. If your activities are well-chosen, public speaking and community involvement can help you become better known as well. For example, the accountant whose field is financial planning should speak on that subject as often as possible.

In the final analysis, being perceived as an expert takes a lot of self-promotion. Do what you can with press releases, and remain alert to the additional opportunities for exposure. Once your reputation begins to grow, you may well find that the press won't leave you alone!

THE PHYSICAL APPEARANCE OF YOUR COMPANY

The look of your office or store is another factor which contributes to the overall perception of your company.

Retail stores have a particular challenge with both window and indoor displays to plan. These are an excellent way of attracting attention for your company, so it's important that they be consistent with the image you want to project. Even if a gourmet store carries common grocery items, these are not the items to be featured in your displays. Try to look at both your interior and exterior displays objectively. Is what they convey to the public part of the image you want to project?

Business owners who work out of offices must make the same evaluation. The office should represent you well. An interior designer who works out of a bare office with old furniture is making a big mistake. Her office should be considered her showroom where she demonstrates her talent for putting together combinations of furniture and floor and wall coverings that work. A client should gain confidence from the physical surroundings where the designer works. The same principle holds true for any other professsional. Do you want your environment to be well-organized? Comfortable? Elegant? Relaxed? See that it's consistent with your image.

THE APPEARANCE OF YOUR STATIONERY AND PRINTED MATERIAL

The first impression you make on someone you meet largely depends on how you look. That's why many businesspeople make an effort to dress in a way that is suitable to their profession. Your stationery and printed material have the same responsibility---

many of you probably <u>first greet potential customers through printed literature</u>, so it's <u>important that the material make a good impression.</u>

If you've not yet had a graphic artist develop a concept for the look of your printed materials, you would be wise to consult one now. This needn't be an expensive venture. You may have a friend who will work with you for a reasonable fee, or try contacting a nearby college for names of art students who might work with you for a price you can afford.

<u>The look of your stationery and logo should be consistent with the type of business you're in.</u> For example, a health food store which projects a back-to-nature image would be wrong to select a fancy, heavily swirled style of type.

Also, remember that in many cases, your written material will be sent to strangers. <u>Don't assume that they will understand something which may have personal meaning</u>. If you own a fabric store and your Siberian husky spends all day with you at the shop, you might have a passing fancy to use a husky logo for your stationery. Don't. A sketch of a husky conveys nothing helpful about your business, and those who don't know you will simply think it's odd. <u>Look for a graphic idenity which expresses who you are.</u>

<u>Strive for a consistency among all your printed material</u>. Your artist may recommend varying the use of color or the use of the design from piece to piece, but be sure that there's still a consistent feel to it. Your brochure should project the same qualities your letterhead does, for example.

Finally, <u>spend what it takes to have your letterhead or brochures printed on a good paper stock</u>. In many cases, your printed material will be the sole item representing you. <u>Make sure it is as good as you and your business are</u>.

YOUR STAFF

Some business owners are natural-born managers, while others rue the day their company grew to a size where staff was required. Whatever your feelings, it cannot be stressed enough that-- second only to you--<u>your staff is highly representative of what kind of company you are</u>.

From an ace salesperson who really knows how to handle a client to the boy at the cash register who says, "Thank you for shopping here," these people represent you directly. With this in mind, you may want to put staff training and improved communications higher on your list of priorities to assure that your employees are projecting the positive image you want. Without good staff management, poor morale, absenteeism and employee turnover can harm you immeasurably.

Of course, the first step in building a good staff is to <u>hire properly in the first place</u>. You're probably better off selecting those applicants who are already projecting an image similar to what you want rather than trying to re-shape someone. In other words, if congeniality is important in your line of work, be sure the new employee you hire is friendly and outgoing by nature.

A happy employee, of course, is likely to be the best

employee. Aside from <u>paying the best wages you can afford,</u>
here are some other advantages you may be able to offer your
employee:

Job Involvement and Enlarged Responsibilities

Workers in large companies often become disinterested in their
work because the particular function to which they are relegated
is so boring. They never feel a part of the total picture of
what the company does.

Most individually owned companies can offer much <u>greater
opportunities for the aggressive person who wants to learn.</u>
When hiring you may be able to attract a good quality of
individual by offering growth and involvement in the job.

Flexibility

This is another advantage a business owner can sometimes
offer. While large companies suffer the pains of instituting
flexitime, <u>smaller businesses can usually work out schedules
which are well-suited to the lifestyles of their employees</u>.

Recognition

Too few supervisors in corporations remember how important
a simple "thank you" can be. <u>Personal attention and recognition</u>
for a job well done is another benefit business owners can
painlessly offer their staffs.

Other management tools usually thought of in connection with
major corporations can be extremely useful to the business owner
who wants the staff to feel they play a part in the company's goals:

Effective Employee Communications

Though it would seem that the small- to medium- size company
would have an easier time communicating with its staff, this
isn't always the case. Time is tight; the workload is heavy,

and there is little opportunity for sitting down to discuss
the company's state of affairs. Yet this type of discussion
can be very important in maintaining good employee morale.
How can they feel involved in their work if they don't understand what's going on in the company as a whole? You might
like to try scheduling an out-of-the-office breakfast or dinner
(probably paying them for the time) in order to keep them
informed. For most businesses this would be time well-spent.

Job Reviews

 Job reviews are usually the province of large corporations,
but it's a good way for any company to communicate with staff
members on a one-to-one basis. By scheduling a regular time for
a job review (perhaps once or twice a year), you can use it as
an opportunity for a two-way exchange. Learn their feelings
about the company, and then let them know how you think they
are progressing. Make your feelings and expectations clear.
You might do well to set some goals together which will satisfy
some of the employee's goals while still being in line with
company aims. If the job review is a favorable one, benefits
other than salary increase which might be offered could be
educational opportunities, a bonus, increased responsibilities
or free time.

Upward Mobility

 Most employees want some form of upward mobility in their
work, and for that reason, you should attempt to promote from
within when possible. If a particular employee is good at his
job but has no other future with your company, you may have to
have a frank discussion with him if he expresses other
expectations. Most staff members will be happier if they have
a general idea of what they can look forward to within the
company.

 Of course, what you're striving for in building a satisfied
staff is the creation of an ideal team. From cashier to

accountant, you can have everyone reflecting a positive company image which will, in turn, translate into a well-satisfied clientele.

PUBLIC RELATIONS AND THE TELEPHONE

For many business owners, the telephone is one of the most important methods of communication with the public. For this reason, it's extremely important that you give careful consideration as to how your business telephone calls are handled.

If you're a one-person operation, be sure to arrange for your phone to be answered even when you're not available. An answering service or an answering machine will do nicely. Then be sure to check for messages and return calls regularly.

If you have only one phone line and find that you are using it a great deal, call your local telephone company. In many parts of the country, the phone company can now install specialized services for a very reasonable fee. "Call waiting" is a system which signals you during a call if you are receiving another incoming call, and it would seem to be particularly handy for business owners who want to avoid missing any calls.

If you have a secretary or a receptionist answering your phone, here are some additional points to keep in mind:

1. If someone asks, "Is Mary Smith in?", the person answering the phone should say "yes" or "no" before asking who is calling. If the question is posed before the caller's question is answered, it makes it seem like whether she's "in" or "out" depends on who the caller is.

2. <u>Try to avoid putting people on hold</u> for very long. If
   a call must be put on hold, be sure to <u>check back</u> with
   the caller <u>periodically</u>.

3. If your receptionist has given the impression that
   you're available, you probably ought to try to take the
   call even if all you say is, "I'm really tied up. May
   I get back to you in an hour?" <u>If you're in a meeting</u>
   <u>or simply prefer not to take calls</u> for a time, <u>your</u>
   <u>receptionist should be told ahead of time.</u>

4. <u>Make any caller feel important</u>, just as you and your staff
   would if you were doing business with them in person.

<u>PUTTING YOUR PUBLICITY TO WORK TO FURTHER YOUR IMAGE</u>

Another aspect of building your image is putting your
publicity to work for you. Reporters, editors, producers
and consumers all have one thing in common--they think
<u>something is more credible if it's in print.</u> Once you
begin to collect press clippings, you'll want to begin using
them to your own advantage.

As discussed earlier, <u>any publicity you get should</u>
<u>become a regular part of the press information you send out.</u>
The clippings may provide supplementary information or
present the material from a different angle which could be
helpful in interesting the press.

Some businesses such as retail stores and restaurants
have <u>newspaper articles or reviews enlarged for display</u>
in the window of the establishment. This can be useful
in attracting new customers who would like to get a flavor

of the place before giving it a try.

Enclosing copies of your press clippings when writing to customers, potential customers and suppliers can also be a good idea. Current customers enjoy the feeling of, "I knew it all along..."; potential customers may be encouraged to give your business a try when they realize you're getting high marks from the press; and suppliers take pride in servicing someone who is well-respected.

Ultimately, the positive image you develop for your company should result in one of the most powerful forms of promotion available: good word-of-mouth.

Chapter XI

HOW AND WHEN TO HIRE AN OUTSIDE PUBLIC RELATIONS FIRM

No matter how successful your own publicity program, there
may come a time when you decide to have someone else handle that
aspect of your business.

What is likely to bring about such a decision? Don't
necessarily expect it to be growth. As a matter of fact, many
companies going through a period of rapid expansion will
simply choose to put a full-time publicist on staff to handle
the increased volume of work.

Then why? You may come to the point where you and the
entire staff are simply too strapped for time. Outside
representation will free you from all but the planning and
the actual media interview hours.

Or you may have been happy with your internal efforts
up to now, but may feel completely tapped out when it comes
time to develop ideas for a new push. An outside pro may
be able to help you come up with some fresh new angles.

Or you may work in a field such as some areas of the
fashion industry where there's even a star system for

publicists. Being accepted as a client by the "right" one
is a public relations coup in itself. In this case, proper
outside representation may enhance your prestige.

Finally, you may have identified one type of story--
perhaps a product listing or a major feature story--which could
really help business take off. If that placement continues
to elude you, then you may want to see if an expert can bring
it in.

But before attempting to select the proper firm, it's
important to identify who within your company will be working
with the public relations professional. This person should be
included in the selection process from the beginning, because
it's important that he or she thoroughly understand the
following:

- How the public relations process works (The Publicity
  Manual explains that.)

- What do you hope to accomplish by going to the outside?

- What type of person will work best with you and your
  team? (This will be discussed in the following section.)

HOW TO SELECT THE BEST FIRM FOR YOUR COMPANY

Selecting outside public relations representation is
a delicate task: This business relationship will be among
your most sensitive, because you are hiring an outsider who
must represent you as if he were an insider. This person should
know you and your company or product inside and out, and he
or she should be adept at conveying your feelings to the
press. You'll have less influence on this person than you

would have on a full-time employee, but if you've hired the proper professional and the chemistry is right, then they'll be able to do a fine job for you.

Word-of-mouth is the best way to begin your search for a good firm. Think about your business associates who get consistently favorable exposure, and ask about who they're using. Better yet, consult some of the reporters whom you've gotten to know and respect. If a writer particularly likes working with one or two publicists, then you might do well to be represented by one of them.

As you begin your investigation, one of your first concerns may be big firm vs. small firm or individual. This is largely a personal choice which will depend on the field you're in and your company's business style.

Specialists in your subject matter may be one of the advantages of a large P.R. firm. If your business is a young brokerage company trying to get a firm foothold, then a large firm will likely have experts who know exactly how to place financial stories. (However, remember that in the P.R. business, knowing how to place a story is quite different from being able to guarantee that it will be done.)

In addition, the large firm will already have established contacts with the type of reporters who might be covering your stories.

For all the pluses a big firm can offer, there will be some drawbacks, too. Consider: Though you may initially meet with an account executive whom you like and admire, are you

sure this is the person who will actually be representing you?
Sometimes contact work is delegated to an underling.

Are the members of your team accessible? If you're a
small account with a very large firm, what kind of service can
you really expect? Do you get right through when you call?
Do they stay in touch with you to let you know the status of
their assignment? (After all, you're paying them!)

Small firms--or even sole practitioners--offer advantages
to consider. When you meet with the account executive, it will
likely be very obvious who is going to do the work for you;
small firms generally don't have much staff to whom to delegate.
You'll likely meet and know everyone who will be working on
your account.

Your success will be their success. If you're a big account
to a small firm, they're going to work even harder for you
to build the credentials they want for themselves. And while
it might be helpful to have a publicist who already knows your
field, it needn't be a requirement. One generalist once
commented, "My motto is, 'What I don't know today, I'll know
tomorrow.'" She knows that if she's successful in representing
a new client, that may lead to more accounts in the field.

Once you narrow your choices enough to begin interviewing,
one of the first things to look for is a successful track
record. At the first interview, a publicist should be prepared
to present various campaigns on which he or she has worked
and display the results of these efforts.

As the discussion turns to your company, you'll want to get a feel as to whether the package they're offering you is one tailor-made for your needs which takes into account your priorities or whether it's a pre-fabricated package they try to sell companies in fields similar to yours.

Also try to judge how hard they want to work on your account. Will they be making separate phone calls for you, or do you think they'll just tack on a "plug" for your product on press calls they are making anyway?

Are you comfortable with the fact that this particular person will represent the company you've worked so hard to build? How did they dress? How did they handle your initial interview? Did they overstay their appointment despite hints from you? If so, they may lack the ability to pick up on small, but important sensitivities. Did they leave before all your questions were answered? Perhaps they're too busy to take on a new client. Did they seem to have a genuine desire to immerse themselves in your field and learn all they can about it?

What you're ultimately seeking is someone with whom you click. Does the publicist like and believe in what you're doing? They'll pitch it better if they do.

WHAT KIND OF FEES CAN YOU EXPECT?

When it comes to projected fees, I can give you only the most general figures. Too much depends on the size and type of business you run and the size and type of public relations firm being considered. In addition, the area of the country in which you work will affect cost.

I would estimate that based on metropolitan area rates the average amount a small business owner should expect to pay is about $1000 a month.

While in the long run a monthly retainer is probably the best arrangement to make with a public relations firm, some may be willing to discuss one-shot projects with you or even agree to a day rate for something special. However, most will prefer the retainer, and some may be unwilling to discuss anything less than a three-month minimum.

In evaluating the expense, you'll need to consider what it costs (factoring in effectiveness) to handle it internally.

And whether you decide to pay $500 or $2500 a month, be sure to select a firm who is promising blue-ribbon service for whatever the agreed-upon fee. If you don't feel terrific about the way your P.R. firm is treating you, then you're with the wrong firm for you money.

An example of this occurred with a market research company whose president decided to stretch the budget a bit in order to afford a firm charging $2000 a month. For the money, they were contacting Good Morning, America, Newsweek, Business Week and Forbes as well as many local programs and publications. Results were relatively good, however, the firm never provided her with any sort of accounting of whom they had contacted or what the reaction had been. This was a serious loss. If she was going to have the "honor" of being rejected by Business Week, she needed to know why in order to formulate a stronger publicity program for the future. After repeated requests for some form of accountability had been ignored, the market research president finally took her business elsewhere and found that a less prestigious firm was able to provide her with better service for less money.

When you begin to discuss cost, your publicist should also be able to discuss priorities. If they've quoted you $1300, yet you'd prefer to spend only $900 per month, could priorities be set on the work involved so that the two of you can continue to do business? Tell them that if they're successful at publicizing you, you'll soon be able to afford their $1300!

In addition to the general fee charged by the firm, some additional expenses are generally passed on to the client. As you discuss thse points, the account executive or publicist should be able to give you average costs on each item for clients of their firm:

Telephone expenses--Sometimes both local and long-distance costs will be passed on. If you're seeking local exposure, this item won't be too high, but if you're based in Houston and hoping for national attention, then your firm will likely be ringing up a lot of long-distance charges.

Entertainment--Lunch with the press is on you!

Printing costs of photos and all print materials.

Postage.

Travel--If the publicist accompanies you on out-of-town trips for media interviews, your company pays all costs.

Once you've struck a business agreement, be sure to
stipulate all you've discussed in a formal letter of agreement.
You should also set an end date for the relationship--or a
date at which the agreement should be re-evaluated. Neither
of you will be happy with an open-ended arrangement.

WHAT RESULTS CAN YOU EXPECT?

What can you expect for your money? An honorable business relationship---that's all. The P.R. professional you
hire should provide you with ideas, help you develop campaigns
and give you a regular report on what contacts they have made
on your behalf. In addition, they should return your phone
calls promptly and give every indication that they are doing
their best for you. Other than that, they cannot--and will not--
guarantee results.

While you--like other business owners--may turn to an outside professional for a particular type of exposure like product
publicity in New York Magazine's "Best Bets" section or an
interview in Fortune, a public relations firm should tell you
at the start that while they will be happy to work toward
that goal for a set period of time, there is no way to guarantee
that you will get the exposure you're after. By the same
token, a good firm will give you a knowledgeable analysis of
how realistic your hopes are.

In this regard, you'll also find that timing is crucial,
and you may want to get some guidelines on this from the
professional with whom you're working. He or she may feel

they'll need six months to a year to work on a certain type
of placement, or they may tell you that within three months
they'll be able to give you an answer.

ESTABLISHING THE RELATIONSHIP

As you begin your relationship, take the time to thoroughly acquaint your publicist with your field and with your
particular operation. If he or she is going to be talking
about the manufacture of videodiscs, then he had better
see the plant, understand the product and know about the
competition. In addition, explain why your product and
company are the best.

Next, sit down and have a good discussion about your
needs and objectives. Many P.R. professionals say that most
trouble begins because a business owner has been unclear as
to what is really important to him. If you were born and raised
in Denver, Colorado and are now running a successful business
in Los Angeles, then you may relish the thought of having a
story about you appear in The Denver Post. Tell the P.R. firm
that! While it might not have been among the outlets they had
planned to approach, it's still a perfectly valid form of
publicity.

From the outset, you should also establish how often you
want to be informed as to how things are going. Once a week?
Once a month? By letter or by phone?

As the P.R. firm begins to set up interviews for you,
you'll also want to be sure the necessary homework is being

done. Now that you or a staff member will no longer be working directly with the press, you'll want to be informed of exactly what the topic is, what the purpose of the interview is and who else the reporter will be talking to. In addition, you'll likely want some information on the writer and his background.

Finally, your last task is to step back and leave the public relations firm alone. After all, you've hired them to free up your time, so now is the opportunity to see how well they can do what they're best at. Give them time and latitude, and they'll almost surely exceed your expectiations.

Resources

RESOURCES

The "Resources" section of the book is included to provide
you with a miscellany of additional helpful information. There
is material on media directories, distribution and clipping services
as well as public relations organizations. Also included is a
chart for tracking your publicity and answers to some of the
more interesting questions I have been asked.

PRESS LIST RESOURCES

As I'm sure you gathered from reading "The Media," there is
no way that The Publicity Manual can provide each reader with a
tailor-made press list to whom you will want to submit your
material. Each person's situation is simply too individual.
Your press list will be determined by your location, the field
in which you work and the type of exposure you're seeking.
What's more, every time you do a new press mailing, your list will
almost surely be a little different from the last time.

What I can do is point you in the right direction for
building your first press list. (Remember to use the index

card system suggested on pages 124-125. That way you can
re-shuffle rather than re-build your list for each mailing.)

Local Print and Broadcast Media
  Your own phone book or--for print--the publication itself
  are the best resources for finding addresses and phone
  numbers.

Regional Print and Broadcast Media
  For print, there's nothing better than a copy of the publication. However, if this isn't readily available then
  check copies of the appropriate telephone books which you'll
  find at your local library or telephone company. The phone
  directories will also give you the addresses and phone numbers
  of the broadcast media.

Trade Publications
  For publications other than the ones you subscribe to,
  Bacon's Publicity Checker, Ayer Directory of Publications
  and Gebbie Press All-in-One Directory (see below) are
  excellent.

National Print and Broadcast Media
  In the accompanying Media Resource Directory I've tried to
  provide you with a sampling of the better-known publications
  and programs. However, the Directory is by no means all-inclusive.
  To obtain addresses of additional national publications, watch
  your local newsstand or bookstore. For radio and television,
  a little dial- or channel-switching will help you assess the
  national radio and television possibilities, and program
  addresses can then be obtained from the local station. You
  might also want to refer to the broadcast directories listed
  below.

Media Directories

There are many excellent directories which provide complete contact information for various media outlets. Addresses, phone numbers, and in some cases, the names of editors and department heads are listed.

The following two directories list all major newspapers (daily and weekly) plus news services and syndicates as well as business, trade and consumer magazines:

> Bacon's Publicity Checker
> 14 East Jackson Blvd.
> Chicago, IL 60604
>
> Ayer Directory of Publications
> Ayer Press
> One Bala Avenue
> Bala Cynwyd, PA 19004

The following includes both print and broadcast media combined:

> Gebbie Press All-in-One Directory
> Box 1000
> New Paltz, N.Y. 12561

These list individual shows according to their location:

> Radio Contacts
> Larimi Communications
> 151 East 50th Street
> New York, N.Y. 10022
>
> TV Contacts
> Larimi Communications
> (as above)

The following supplies nationwide TV information and will sell single pages of the directory to provide information on specific cities:

> TV Publicity Outlets
> P.O. Box 327
> Washington Depot, CT 06794

Specialized directories such as the following for syndicated columnists and the one for newsletters can also be invaluable. Remember that newsletters can have a great degree of credibility with their readers, so a special effort to mail to appropriate publications can be well worth your time!

Syndicated Columnists
Richard Weiner, Inc.
888 Seventh Avenue
New York, N.Y. 10019

The Newsletter Yearbook Directory
The Newsletter Clearinghouse
44 West Market Street
Rhinebeck, N.Y. 12572

Several major cities also have directories for the media in the area:

Metro California Media   (metropolitan areas in
Public Relations Plus, Inc.   the state)
P.O. Box 327
Washington Depot, CT 06794

New York Publicity Outlets
Public Relations Plus, Inc.
P.O. Box 327
Washington Depot, CT 06794

Greater Philadelphia Pulbicity Guide
Fund Raising Institute
Box 365
Ambler, PA   19002

Hudson's Washington News Media Contacts Directory
2626 Pennsylvania Avenue, N.W.
Washington, DC 20037

Connecticut Media Directory
Maryland/Delaware Media Directory
New England Media Directory
New Jersey Media Directory
New York State Media Directory
Pennsylvania Media Directory
Burrelle's Media Directories
75 East Northfield Avenue
Livingston, N.J. 07039

You might want to consider investing in one directory. They tend to be expensive ($40-90), and new editions are issued annually. However, one book should provide you with addresses and phone numbers which would remain accurate for several years. (Only the names would out-date quickly, and they do anyway.)

If you're not prepared to make the investment now, check with your local library. They may have a copy of one of the books or could order one for you. Or perhaps the librarian could refer you to a similar book which will give you all the information you need.

OTHER AIDS

Newsletter

"Party Line" is a weekly newsletter read by P.R. professionals. The media uses it to notify publicists of their needs (Working Woman may announce that they have a new articles editor, or Family Circle may request new craft ideas for an upcoming issue, for example.) Annual subscriptions run about $90, but some of the information is quite good. Maybe someone would share a subscription with you. Send for a sample copy:

"Party Line"
P.R. Aids
330 West 34th Street
New York, N.Y. 10001

Distribution Services

These services will print and mail your press releases for you. For around $30 plus postage, a service will mail out

100 one-page releases to a computerized list of your choice.

This might be helpful for a large mailing, but remember that throughout this book we've discussed how important the "personal touch" is in getting publicity. Be sure to weigh the merits of this against the minus of using a computerized list before thinking seriously of using a distribution service.

If interested, two services to price are:

P.R. Aids
330 West 34th Street
New York, N.Y. 10001

(212) 947-7733

Bacon's Publicity Distribution Service
14 East Jackson Blvd.
Chicago, IL 60604

(312) 922-8419

Clipping Services

If you are generating a great deal of publicity, then you might want to consider a clipping service. However, they are expensive (with a per clipping and a per month charge), and thoroughness can be a problem until your name becomes relatively well-known. Keep in mind that you may request clipping of statewide or regional publications only.

Bacon's Clipping Service
14 East Jackson Blvd.
Chicago, IL 60604

Burrelle's Press Clipping Service
75 East Northfield Avenue
Livingston, N.J. 07039

Luce Press Clipping Service
420 Lexington Avenue
New York, N.Y. 10017

Public Relations Organizations

There are independent publicity clubs in New York City, Boston, Los Angeles, San Diego, San Francisco and Northbrook, Illinois. Some run excellent courses on publicity. If you live near one of these cities, check your phone book and call for information.

In addition, the Public Relations Society of America has chapters nationwide. In Manhattan, the PRSA has an excellent library which is open to the public. Contact the New York office for chapters in your area:

    The Public Relations Society of America
    845 Third Avenue
    New York, N.Y. 10017
    (212) 826-1750

SAMPLE CHART FOR TRACKING YOUR PUBLICITY

You can use a chart like this one (there's a blank copy on the following page) to keep track of your releases.

Each chart should represent the progress of a separate release. Simply fill in the publications and contacts to whom the material was sent as well as when you follow up and what the status of the story is.

On the following sample chart, note that because this business owner offered an exclusive to columnists at the Times and New York, she sent out no other releases until after the New York piece appeared.

Sample Chart

Release Info: "New Service" Release

Media	Contact	Date Sent	Follow-up Call	Status
New York Times	(name) "Discoveries" column OFFERED EXCLUSIVE	7/6	7/12	not interested
New York Mag.	(name) "Best Bets" column-OFFERED EXCLUSIVE	7/13	7/20	will run in August 15 issue!
NY Daily News	(name) "You" section	8/22	8/30	"under con- sideration"
Our Town (neighborhood newspaper)	(name) Editor	8/22	8/30	liked idea. Gav release to writer who wil call for inter- view.
Channel 4 News	(name) consumer reporter	8/22	8/31	Call back in 3 weeks
AM New York (TV talk show)	(name) producer	9/3	9/10	interview set for Oct. 4
WOR Radio	(name) producer	9/3	9/10	Will call if interested at later date
Venture Mag. (monthly mag.)	(name) Managing Editor	9/3	9/15	interested-- needs picture

TRACKING YOUR PUBLICITY

Release Info: _____ Release

Media	Contact	Date Sent	Follow-up Call	Status

FREQUENTLY ASKED QUESTIONS

    In the process of teaching publicity techniques, I have the opportunity to hear many types of questions. Here are some that are asked most frequently:

Approaching the Competition

Q: I live in a two-newspaper town, and one of the newspapers did a story about me several months ago. How long should I wait before trying to get publicity in the competing paper?

A: You needn't wait any time at all. The fact that you have gotten publicity in one paper proves that you are of interest locally. You're right in thinking that the competing paper won't want to write the exact same story about you, so start trying to interest them in a new story angle you've developed. Remember, it's mainly the columnists who want total exclusivity on their stories, and even they would be interested in hearing from you if you've got a new story angle for them.

    Incidentally, if you've "created" news by sponsoring a special event, for example, you should definitely try to get publicity in both papers at the same time. You're current news. If one paper uses the story on Monday, you should still encourage the other paper to use the story later in the week.

Multiple Submissions

Q: May I send more than one release on the same subject to different people at the same publication?

A: I advise against this. Multiple submissions of the release may actually dampen their enthusiasm. If one reporter notes that you've sent it to someone else as well (and you should always explain if you've sent multiple copies), then that reporter may think, "Oh well, so-and-so will probably cover it..." and throw it away. Or if you should be fortunate enough to interest both reporters in the story, then you've

created an internal problem for them: they have to decide who
is going to do the story.

If time permits, the best way to handle this situation is
to send a release to one person at a publication at a time. Then
follow up with a phone call. If they aren't interested, you can
then send the release to someone else.

Will Ad Dollars Lead to Publicity?

Q: Will buying ads help me get publicity?

A: Definitely not with major publications. The ad department and
the editorial department operate completely independently.

Small publications will sometimes offer an editorial blurb on
your company if you buy space for an ad--you'll particularly
see this arrangement where neighborhood restaurants and boutiques
are concerned. However, these publications are usually very
direct about what they are offering you, so it's not being used
as a subtle way to trick you into buying an ad.

Less reputable publications may try to tell you that buying
an ad in the newspaper or magazine will guarantee you editorial
space. This isn't a particularly good practice. If you are
approached on this basis, you'll just have to evaluate whether
it's worth it to you.

Publicity as a Last-ditch Effort

Q: I've just started a business, and my advertising isn't doing
    for me what I had hoped it would. If I don't get some free
    publicity within the next couple of months I'll have to go
    out of business. How can I get started?

A: This is a question I've been hearing frequently, and it has
disturbed me greatly. Now that you've read The Publicity Manual,
I'm sure you realize that there is no way you can control when
or if you'll get publicity in a certain publication. For this
reason, I always feel so badly to think that publicity efforts which
may pay off handsomely in six months won't do this person any
good because they may have to go out of business within the next two.

However, just recently a woman who originally posed this question to me proved that my concern for her was unnecessary. Three months ago she took my publicity workshop saying that without exposure through publicity she just couldn't keep her business going much longer. She asked, how could she get an article in The New York Times or The Daily News within the next month or two? In the workshop, I did all I could for her, and at the conclusion, all I could do was wish her luck.

Well, she didn't quite make her deadline of "the next month or two," but it's now been three months since I first met her, and she has been written about twice in The Daily News--and one of those articles was a 2½-page spread totally dedicated to her and her business! What about The Times? Oh, she was interviewed for an article there, and that piece is to appear sometime this month!

There's no miracle story about how she accomplished this-- she simply took the techniques learned in the workshop and added one other ingredient: time. Because she wasn't busy with clients, she devoted approximately 50 percent of her work week to her publicity program--a very intelligent move since she was counting on publicity to save her business. She set a goal, learned the techniques needed to accomplish it, and then devoted the time and energy to seeing it through. I think she's going to be in business a long, long time.

Though I still prefer to see publicity viewed as part of an overall business plan rather than a last-ditch effort to save a business, this story proves that with dedication and a little luck it can be done!

What About Results?

Q: How much business can you expect from publicity?

A: That's a very difficult question to answer, because there are so many variables involved. It depends on the publication and its audience as well as the type of article.

Obviously, if you're quoted in passing, you probably won't get as much business as you would if an entire article is devoted to you.

And to illustrate the difficulty of predicting how you'll fare in various publications, I can give you an example from my experience publicizing <u>The Publicity Manual</u>. From a blurb in a very good magazine for entrepreneurs with a circulation of about 75,000 we received approximately 25 orders--an excellent response, we thought. However, a similar write-up in a trade newsletter with a circulation half the size of the magazine brought in over 250 orders! Who could have predicted it? I certainly wouldn't have. Obviously, the newsletter has excellent credibility with its readers, and a recommendation there was a very significant one.

But regardless of exactly how much business a piece of publicity brings, remember that every time you're written about or interviewed it adds to your credibility.

Print Publicity vs. Broadcast Publicity

Q: Is print publicity more effective than broadcast publicity?

A: In general, you'll usually find that print publicity has the advantage of being something that can be clipped and saved. If a woman reads about you while commuting to work by train, she can save the article and may call you days or months later. If she's driving to work and hears an interview with you on the radio, it will be somewhat more difficult. Though she may later remember your name and what you were talking about, she probably won't have the opportunity to pull to the side of the road and write down enough information that she'll want to file and save it for future reference.

But again, it's difficult to generalize. One business owner had a nice 2½-minute segment devoted to her business on a TV news program. To her surprise, she received only one phone call as a result of that publicity. However, that one client hired her for a long-term project which kept her busy for several weeks. Though the business owner might have been disappointed in the number of calls, she certainly wasn't upset about the volume of work which resulted!

Press Conferences

Q: What about press conferences?

A: If your message can be conveyed in a press release, press
kit or in one-to-one meetings scheduled at the convenience of
individual reporters, these methods are preferable to holding
a press conference. The media have difficulty finding time to
attend pre-arranged conferences on anything but the most
earth-shaking news. And of course, the risk to you is that if
you hold a press conference on a marginal story, they may not
attend.

However, if you are involved in an ongoing "front page" story
where immediate answers are important, if there is controversy
over your issue or if there may be need for a two-way discussion
between media and spokesperson, then a press conference may be
appropriate. If so, refer to page 51 for reminders on timing such
an event. Next, hand-deliver press releases announcing the
conference, prepare press kits and rehearse your spokespeople.
Immediately before the conference, make reminder phone calls to
the media (If they can't attend, offer to send follow-up material
about what was discussed.) and on that day, have someone on
hand to greet the press and see to their needs. Afterward,
phone or send follow-up information to the media who did not
attend.

Cracking a Tough Publication

Q: I just can't seem to get publicity in one particular
    publication. What can I do?

A: Be persistent! Try a different editor or reporter, and
think of new story angles. Getting publicity in one specific
publication can take time, but in all likelihood, you'll be
able to crack it. In the meantime, keep working to get your
name in the publications where you seem to have easier access.

Ethics and Experience

Q: My partner and I have just started a new type of counseling
    service, and I recently suggested an article about it to a
    major newspaper. The reporter loved the idea, interviewed us
    and also talked to our competitors. The only thing which
    caught us off guard was when she asked to meet some of the
    clients for whom we've achieved satisfactory results. Though
    we have clients, none have been with us long enough to have
    finished the program, so we were unable to give her any names.
    Finally, the article appeared and to our great disappointment,
    we weren't mentioned. When I called to ask why, the reporter
    said it was because we had no track record. But the article
    idea was ours, was this fair?

A: That's a difficult question. You were all in an awkward spot.
You didn't realize that she would want to interview clients and
so you were unprepared; she was stuck because she had to complete
her assignment despite your situation. And in honesty to her
readers, she probably worried about recommending you when she had
no opportunity to verify your reputation (as she must have had
with your competitors).

    I think the lesson to be learned here is to always be prepared
to back your credibility. A graphic artist may donate artwork
initially simply to have proof that his work is being used (no
one need know it wasn't paid for). In your case, do you have
former clients whom you counseled prior to starting the business
who could have talked to the reporter about your effectiveness?
Those clients may not have come to you under your current business
name, but if you helped them solve a similar problem, then their
comments would be perfectly valid. I think business owners should
be aware of the fact that they may need to substantiate their claims
with satisfied customers. You may want to hold off on publicity
until you have people who can vouch for you--even if it's only
a friend for whom you worked for free.

"Off the Record"

Q: What does speaking to a reporter "off the record" mean?

A: If you tell a reporter that something is "off the record,"
it means that he is bound by honor not to quote you as the source

of the remark. He may use the information directly or indirectly in the article, but your name will not be attached to it.

Try to avoid saying that something is "off the record." If there is something you'd prefer not to have known, it's a better idea not to discuss it at all.

Survey Articles vs. Profile Pieces

Q: A particular magazine where I would like to get publicity usually does survey articles including several businesses of the same type. They rarely focus on one individual business. If I send them my press release and they like it, is there a way to encourage them to profile my business rather than writing a survey article which will surely include my competitors?

A: No, I don't think they will change the format of the magazine for this one article. However, there's reason to reconsider your attitude. If the magazine is a successful one, then they've probably determined that survey articles are popular with readers--that they are read and saved by a good number of individuals. In this case, response to the article may well be so healthy that it wouldn't hurt that much to share some of the publicity "wealth" with your competitors. Also, remember that you will--or may have already--benefited from your competitors' efforts to gain media exposure. One business owner noted of her competitors: "I don't worry if they are included in the same article I am. What's good for one of us always ends up being good for all of us."

*   *   *

At the beginning of The Publicity Manual I recommended that you read the book straight through before settling down to write your first press release. Now I assume that you have finished your first reading, and I urge you to go right back to "The Basics" and begin to outline your own publicity program.

These methods can and do work. Give them a try!